TORONTO'S
RAVINES

TORONTO'S RAVINES

WALKING THE HIDDEN COUNTRY

Murray Seymour

The BOSTON
MILLS PRESS

CATALOGING IN PUBLICATION DATA

Seymour, Murray, 1936–
Toronto ravines : walking the hidden country

ISBN 1-55046-322-5

1. Trails — Ontario — Toronto
— Guidebooks. 2. Gorges — Ontario
— Toronto — Guidebooks. 3. Walking —
Ontario — Toronto — Guidebooks. I. Title.

FC3097.18.S495 2000   917.13' 541044
C00-930499-1
F1059.5.T683S495 2000

Published in 2000 by
BOSTON MILLS PRESS
132 Main Street
Erin, Ontario N0B 1T0
Tel 519-833-2407
Fax 519-833-2195
e-mail books@bostonmillspress.com
www.bostonmillspress.com

An affiliate of
STODDART PUBLISHING CO. LIMITED
34 Lesmill Road
Toronto, Ontario, Canada
M3B 2T6
Tel 416-445-3333
Fax 416-445-5967
e-mail gdsinc@genpub.com

Distributed in Canada by
GENERAL DISTRIBUTION SERVICES LIMITED
325 Humber College Boulevard
Toronto, Canada M9W 7C3
Orders 1-800-387-0141 Ontario & Quebec
Orders 1-800-387-0172 NW Ontario
& other provinces
e-mail cservice@genpub.com

Distributed in the United States by
GENERAL DISTRIBUTION SERVICES INC.
PMB 128, 4500 Witmer Industrial Estates,
Niagara Falls, New York 14305-1386
Toll-free 1-800-805-1083
Toll-free fax 1-800-481-6207
e-mail gdsinc@genpub.com
www.genpub.com

Design by Mary Firth
Cover design by Gillian Stead and Mary Firth
Photographs by Murray Seymour
Map drawings by Murray Seymour and
Mary Firth
Printed in Canada

THE CANADA COUNCIL | LE CONSEIL DES ARTS
FOR THE ARTS | DU CANADA
SINCE 1957 | DEPUIS 1957

We acknowledge for their financial support of our
publishing program the Canada Council, the
Ontario Arts Council, and the Government of Canada
through the Book Publishing Industry
Development Program (BPIDP).

CONTENTS

FINDING THE HIDDEN
COUNTRY

Toronto is flat city.

Well yes, there is one hill: Casa Loma sits on it.

Someone given to quibbling might argue that further north the land starts rolling, but let's be honest — it's a flat kind of roll. With all its attractions and delights, in truth, Toronto is flat.

If you've come to the city by air, you've seen it—a little pimple of downtown office towers, with the occasional apartment building pillar sticking up here and there, and of course lots and lots of trees. But flat.

What's hidden below the level of the buildings and the plain are the ravines.

For most, the country hidden in Toronto's ravines is the city's best-kept secret. Oh yes, rumours abound, but when it comes right down to it, where are the darned things? There are green patches on maps, but when you get to where you believe they are, there's an expressway, or a 15-metre vertical cliff, or just a sea of leaves at the back end of the park.

If you were born here, you may have part of the secret. You may well remember your first taste of wilderness, wandering into a green, scary, exciting and probably forbidden place down below. There may have been water, and certainly steep banks, squirrels, and birds. There was a place to build a fort, to hide, to stalk. But even though you remember it today, it may be impossible to find that magic place again.

I stumbled on the secret almost literally by accident.

When I brought my family back to Toronto, after living further north for a while, we didn't have access to a car. Like many Torontonians, I had grown up in a small town, and in the fields and on the lake where my family owned a summer cottage. For much of my adult life I had lived on Toronto Island, and had come to know boats and Lake Ontario in all its moods and guises. But never before had I lived in a suburban high-rise, and the experience was traumatic.

One day in desperation, tired beyond measure of walking the endless paved roadways of suburbia, I cut across an overgrown field and almost fell into a green, riverine land. I remember even now how I felt my chest expand, breathing in the oxygen from the trees. There was water down below, rushing over stones and darting through rapids. It sounded like water, looked like water, smelled like water. And though there was not a cloud in the sky, my cheek was wet.

I had not died and gone to heaven. I'd just found the secret, the real world that has always existed beneath the concrete and glass of the exhaust-fumed, deafening city. I had discovered that which makes this city of Toronto both unique and human, which gives us the chance to reconnect with our roots, quite literally. The ravine lands: the hidden country.

In the years since that day, my wife and I have explored this sunken haven from one end of the city to the other, wherever public transit would take us. We are exploring it still, experiencing newness, wonder, awe and the thrill of discovery, and understanding more about ourselves and about that world underlying all the concrete and steel that we think of as reality.

Over the years, many changes have been made in the name of improving parkland. Most, as we now see with twenty/twenty hindsight, were deleterious to plants, animals, man, and the environment in general. But despite this, the park spaces survived and multiplied and are preserved for us today. And for this we should be profoundly grateful.

In the past few years, the city has begun to reveal some of its green secrets. The ravines have become a popular place to send cyclists and inline skaters to get them off the streets. Paved paths have been built and extended through many

parklands, including the ravines, making them accessible not only to wheels, but also to people with small children, physically challenged people needing a firm, dry place to walk, and thousands of others who want to picnic, char some meat, and chase a soccer ball on a summer afternoon.

The purpose of this book is to make at least some of the literally hundreds of walks in Toronto available to those who want the experience.

And there are still places and trails right in the heart of Toronto that aren't fit for wheels. They may be muddy at times, difficult to climb or descend in places—even a touch dangerous. Most of the walks in this book are concerned with those. They are for hikers, walkers, lovers, kids, amateur naturalists, birders, idlers, romantics, explorers, and those just wanting to walk off Thanksgiving dinner.

The descriptions proceed from west to east, progressing from areas that are more urban and "civilized" to those that are "wild," and from vegetation of a southern kind to that of a more northerly variety.

All walks are accessible by public transport, although a couple in the Rouge Watershed have limited or no service on one or both weekend days. To be sure, check with the TTC (that's short for the Toronto Transit Commission, operator of the city's bus, streetcar and subway systems). All the walks are end-to-end, although some can be looped, so unless you have someone to drop you off and pick you up by car it's easiest to go TTC.

Each walk includes an approximate distance, but be aware that distance is not necessarily an indicator of time. For one thing, you can begin a 4-kilometre walk and be side-tracked by any one of a number of pleasant experiences having the power to consume most of your daylight hours. For another, 7 kilometres along a flat, clear path is different from 7 kilometres through brush, and up and down steep hills and gullies. Read the description to get an idea of what you may be in for along the way.

Note: The person who finishes any one of these walks in the shortest time . . . has missed the whole point, and a lot of other good stuff too! Enjoy.

FOREWORD

Before you lock the door...

In the same way you check to make sure the key is in your pocket before you close the door, take a brief look at some things worth remembering before starting on the walks themselves.

The first safety consideration is for women. This is a subject of relevance in just about any city, but compared with many other places in North America, Toronto has safe parks. Having said that, out of the millions of people in the area there are bound to be a few troubled ones.

Stay out of the parks at night. Some women will not enter parks alone at any time, even to walk their dogs.

I think there are differences between the wilder parks of Highland Creek and the Rouge and those in more urban parts of the city. Contrary to common sense, I think "wilder" in this case is safer, but this is admittedly the view of a large male. Do what feels right for you.

A reasonable concern for safety is not just a female issue—everyone should give at least brief thought to it. Although walking these trails is usually more fun, and safer, when done with someone else, there are times when everyone needs to be alone for a while. But bear in mind that even in the heart of the city, accidents can and do happen. If you're alone when you come to a steep bank, an ice-covered stream, or other potential hazard, ask yourself, "What could happen if...?" Does anyone else know where you've gone or when you'll be back? How far are you from frequently travelled paths or roads? Could a misstep or slip land you in freezing, or deep and fast-moving water? Could you twist an ankle or break a limb? It's easy to do given the right conditions, so always be sure that at least one other person knows where you've gone, even if it's just the landlady.

High water can drown you. In Toronto, the combination of topography and urban structures is such that creek and river levels can rise a metre or more overnight, and what yesterday was a harmless little stream may today be a torrent. There are places and times when neither a child nor an adult can survive a fall into rampaging water, so never underestimate its power.

Hypothermia is the condition that occurs when the core body temperature drops below its usual operating level. If the condition is severe and prolonged, it can kill you, although that's not likely to happen in ravine parks unless drugs, alcohol, or an incapacitating injury are involved.

Most synthetic materials lose moisture quickly. Wool holds it and actually gets warmer. Cotton also holds moisture—whether produced by your body or nature—forever. And there's nothing like soggy cotton to make you cold. Even sweating can chill you badly, so try to wear something other than cotton next to your skin most times of the year.

There's an old belief that if your feet are warm and dry, the rest of you will be too, and there's much truth in that. An extra pair of socks can make all the difference between enjoyment and misery in an afternoon's stroll or a daylong hike. Carry a spare T-shirt and socks at least.

Learn to recognize and avoid both poison ivy and nettles. If you've contacted them before, you'll be very aware of the danger. If you haven't, you don't want to find out! By far the more dangerous of the two is poison ivy, as its effects can last for weeks. After a brush with either, find some jewelweed, crush it, and rub the juice on affected areas. It truly helps.

There are wild animals in the ravines, and looking for them is part of the fun of going there. Other than mosquitoes and little cinnamon-coloured ants, it's not very likely that anything will bite you. However, beware. If any wild animal (other than squirrels in parks and sometimes chickadees) comes towards you, back off. Some animals have become habituated to people, especially if they are fed regularly, and may be regular visitors at your back door. But wild animals are wild.

The greatest danger is from raccoons, foxes, skunks, or coyotes that have contracted rabies. If any of these animals approaches you or acts strangely, move away, and definitely keep children well away. It would be a public service to others, and could possibly even save a life, if you reported such an encounter to the public health department, at (416)-224-6777.

STUFF TO TAKE

For a morning's or afternoon's walk you really don't need much of anything special. If you're going to spend the better part of a day out walking around, you'll probably appreciate a sandwich and some water. The list that follows is optional, but most of the things suggested can add greatly to your enjoyment of the surroundings. However, don't try to take them all.

- Money, keys and TTC tokens or tickets: At some TTC stations you need a transfer to pass from the bus into the subway system. Always get a transfer.
- Medicine: If you're allergic to anything, it's probably out there somewhere. If you are subject to a condition requiring medication at a certain time or for emergencies, take it along. Sometimes activities can take longer than expected, or you miss a bus home, so if there's one chance in a thousand you might need it, take it!
- A backpack: To carry all these other things in!
- Plastic rain cape: They're cheap, light, and will keep you fairly dry until you reach the parking lot or bus stop. You can also use them between yourself and a snow-covered log or wet bit of ground.
- Water: Either tap or bottled, water is better than juice or pop on a hot day. Carry lots of water in summer. You'll appreciate an insulated canteen when temperatures are extreme.
- Food: Nibbles are welcome any time of year; something more substantial is a good idea if you're going to be out during your normal lunch hour. Steaming soup or a hot drink can be wonderful on a raw, wet November day.
- Hat, sunblock, sunglasses: That ol' UV, it ain't what it used to be. Never mind the cumulative effects over the years—a sunburn or a splitting headache from eye strain is painful and unnecessary.
- Bug spray: May to September, it's reassuring to have a little something in the backpack that bugs find offensive. June and July, it's just about mandatory, especially close to the lake along the Rouge River and Highland Creek. Trying to outrun a swarm of mosquitoes in a field of dog strangling vine gives a whole new meaning to the word panic.

- Suitable footwear: If you're just going out once to see if you like it, anything except sandals will do. If you walk (and climb and scramble) a lot, get a good-fitting, well-built, comfortable pair of shoes or boots. Hint: Get a pair of nylon or silk socks and always wear them next to your skin. They transfer moisture, and, because they're slippery, they greatly help in the prevention of blisters caused by friction. Plain old clunky rubber boots can also open up huge wetland areas for you.
- Clothing: Long-sleeved shirts will protect you from UV rays, mosquitoes, poison ivy, nettles and thistles. Slacks do the same for your legs, and also guard against ticks and raspberry vines. Beware, though: mosquitoes love black—it's so sexy.
- Binoculars: If you've got 'em, take 'em. If you don't, make sure that you're feeling really deprived and frustrated before investing in them. Generally, 7x35, wide-angle are recommended.
- Hand lens/magnifier: If you've reached a certain age, you probably have one of these anyway to read telephone books and some maps. But whatever your age, a hand lens can be as valuable as binoculars, and a good deal less expensive.
- Maps: Streets, TTC and bicycle route maps; they don't take up much room. Just keep them permanently in your backpack.
- Guidebooks: Information on birds, plants, fungi, grasses and sedges, bugs, trees, wildflowers, dead plants in winter, scats and tracks, or anything else that catches your fancy. Perhaps start with only one.
- Camera: Anything that you have and like to use. If you want to get started, consider used equipment; all the larger camera stores carry trade-ins. The product—the picture—has its value, but equally or even more rewarding is the process of focussing on, studying, and coming to know some silly little bug or wildflower.
- Sketch pad, journal, tape recorder: As above.

And last, but by no means least....

- Common sense: If it looks dangerous for you, don't do it. If you're cold and wet, get warm and dry. If you're lost, follow a stream and you'll find a road. If you need help, ask for it.

The most important thing to take with you is something that perhaps you've not used since you were very young—an openness to wonder and the ability to suspend disbelief and be amazed. Read on.

CHAPTER 1

THE ETOBICOKE CREEK
WATERSHED

"Is it a creek or a river?" It used to be called a river, and if you see it in the spring or after a heavy rain, it certainly looks like one. However, if you see it any other time of year, it looks more like a creek. Some summers it most closely resembles a series of puddles.

And that's been the whole problem. Like the other rivers in Toronto's watersheds, when it's wet, it's very, very wet, and when it's dry, it's a muddy ditch.

Currently, probably the most important social function of the Etobicoke is to form part of the boundary between Toronto and Mississauga, and how that came about is rather interesting.

The English had replaced the French in the area, and the Town of York was expanding. More settlers were wanted, so the British governor-in-chief, one Lord Dorchester, decided in 1787 that the right thing to do was to buy some land from the current inhabitants. The "Toronto Purchase" was to extend from the west end of the Scarborough Bluffs west to the Etobicoke Creek, the east and west boundaries extending generally north for almost 50 kilometres.

But there was to be one proviso: "Chiefs, Warriors and People of the Mississauga Nation" expressly reserved for their own use "the fishery in the said River Tobicoke." Those chiefs, warriors and people may not have been too aware of the value of money, but they certainly understood the wealth in good fishing. The cost was to be £1,700 plus "much merchandise." That was the intent, but as in many negotiations between peoples of different cultures since time immemorial, it didn't work out quite that way.

The deal was to be done around a three-day council fire near the Bay of Quinte, in September 1787. Everybody concerned showed up and brought along family and friends to enjoy the fun. There were lots of speeches on both sides, and an agreement was reached. Then, as was the custom, came the exchange of gifts. This included all the usual beads and rifles and frying pans, the £1,700, plus 90 gallons of good English rum. Now, in the middle of a party, who wants to be bothered with niggling details like writing all this stuff down on paper?

The next morning. . . .

The English said the west boundary of the purchase was to be the meeting of the Etobicoke River with Lake Ontario.

The Mississauga said the west boundary was to be the Toronto (Humber) River.

But the natives were the owners, and the English...well, the English were English, so it took eighteen years, but at last both sides met again at the Credit River to patch things up. The rum was kept under lock and key this time. The Mississauga accepted ten shillings, "in good and lawful money," as a face-saving gesture, and the deed was finally done. The disputed area between the two rivers, later known as Etobicoke, has since been reputed to have been purchased for 10 shillings, "And worth every penny too."

There was also some dispute as to the spelling of the name. The first attempt was "Wah-do-be-kaug." Others included "Ato-be-coake," "A-doo-be-Kog," "Tobi-coak," and even "Toby Cook." Governor Simcoe didn't much favour the names used by the original inhabitants—they weren't English. So like Adam, he set about naming everything he saw in a civilized tongue, and wanted to call the stream Smith River. But in this decision, at least, the governor did not have the final word, and everybody else continued using their own forms of the original name.

Getting back to the flood and drought problem for a moment, the text of a news report from an earlier time serves to describe the flooding very clearly.

Brampton
TIMES EXTRA!
Friday, August 28, 1857

Immense Fall of Rain! Brampton Flooded!

LAST NIGHT such an immense fall of rain took place, that, early this morning, the River Etobicoke rushed down with fearful velocity, and so overspread its banks, that the greater portion of Brampton was flooded. Through the two railway bridges the water rushed into the principal streets, which were soon like rapid rivers. The water, in several places in the village, was above five feet deep. It went in at the windows of some houses. The damage done is considerable. The planks and sidewalks of some of the streets have been torn up, and small bridges in the neighbourhood carried away. One house has been thrown on one side by the violence of the torrent. Business has been entirely suspended. The flood is now decreasing rapidly; so by tomorrow, we expect Brampton will assume its usual appearance. It is acknowledged by all that this very unexpected immersion of our village is the worst yet experienced.

In consequence of our office having been, like many others, injured by the flood, we will be unable to publish the Weekly Times until Monday next.

Of course, what was true for Brampton, which lies just north of today's Toronto, was equally true of the rest of the watershed. Brampton eventually solved most of the problem by putting the stream in a concrete ditch and leading it around town, but nobody else seemed to get the message that floods were going to recur and were potentially very dangerous.

In the village of Long Branch, where the stream flowed into Lake Ontario, people began to build in the floodplain of the Etobicoke in the 1930s; first cottages, and then homes. The process sped up after the Second World War because of a housing shortage. In the flood of '48, houses were washed away, and twenty people, including mothers and babies, had to be rescued by boat. Yet no government took action, and nobody wanted to leave home and start all over again.

As was true elsewhere in Toronto, it took Hurricane Hazel in 1954 and the consequent loss of seven lives to finally move federal, provincial, Toronto and Long Branch village governments, acting cooperatively, to pay people for their homes so they could find new ones elsewhere. The level of the now-vacant land was raised, and the whole place became a park, as it remains today.

Both Etobicoke and Mimico Creeks are good places to look for fossils in the slabs of grey shale that form most of the creek beds.

Much of the stream is now hemmed in by industry, and there's not a lot of nature left. However there are a number of people dedicated to preserving as much as possible. We can be grateful that at least some of the former wilderness beauty has been retained. The one walk that follows will reveal a little of the former glory of this watershed.

ETOBICOKE WALK 1
CENTENNIAL

DISTANCE: 4 kilometres

NOTE: This is a short and easy walk, mostly through parkland and riverine flats. It's mostly dry.

GETTING THERE BY PUBLIC TRANSPORT: From the Eglinton West Subway Station, take the 32B bus west to the end of the line at Explorer Drive. Cross Eglinton to the south side, and turn left to the entrance to Centennial Park. Follow the road to the parking lot.

GETTING THERE BY AUTOMOBILE: Drive west on Eglinton Avenue past Commerce Boulevard, turn at the sign for Centennial Park announcing the presence of cricket pitches and tennis courts, and continue into the parking lot.

SUMMARY: The walk follows a small, unnamed stream south through Centennial Park almost to the south edge, then west, along the side of a young forest, to Etobicoke Creek. Continue along the top of the creek at first, then through riverine land beside the creek to Burnhamthorpe Road Bridge.

THE WALK: The most obvious landmark is the ski hill, rising straight in front, festooned as it is with lift pylons and floodlights, but this park tends towards flatness. It's covered with hectares of mown lawns, with trees scattered liberally throughout.

For those walking towards the parking lot, there's a little wetland to the right. In the spring it's gloriously populated by male red-winged blackbirds staking out their territories.

From the parking lot, walk along between the wetland and a line of trees, parallel to Eglinton Avenue. Continue heading west until there's a very definite right-angled turn left.

In a pond that's surrounded by purple loosestrife and cattails, there's a small sign on a pole in the middle. Using binoculars you can see that it reads, in small, neat capital letters, No Water Activities Permitted. Now if the dogs would only read and obey small signs, waterfowl could dabble unmolested. Just follow along beside the ponds.

At the last bridge, pause for a moment to look back upstream: it's classically picturesque.

Cross over the bridge towards the washrooms (open in the warmer months), and a parking lot. Continue to Elmcrest Road and then across the field on the other side. Bear to the right (north) towards the end of the line of trees ahead.

Up to the right are various sports installations. On the gravel road, straight ahead, is a stone and concrete bridge, and to the right, a series of ponds and waterfalls created from large slabs of stone and planted around with shrubs and water plants. There's another small wooden footbridge at the top. It's a pleasant place to rest, perhaps have a snack, and let the sound of falling water drown out other auditory distractions.

Further along, after topping a rise, there's a big pond. It often sports a flock of geese spreading across both its surface and the surrounding lawn.

Bear to the left around the end of the woods, head over to Centennial Park Boulevard, then look for the sign pointing to the Centennial Park Composting Site. You're certainly going to hit all the high spots today!

Walking up the left side of the road towards the site, keep an eye open for trucks. Just before reaching the gate, there's a section to the left surrounded on three sides by a low stone wall. Walk to the left corner, and climb over it to find a wide, clear path leading to the edge of a small but deep ravine falling down towards Etobicoke Creek.

Dip down into a wooded area beside the ravine, until you come to the top of the old bank. The trail now leads along the edge of the bank, through the middle of a long, skinny woods.

Continue past the apartment buildings and backyards to a green-painted metal stair structure going down to the newly emerged flat area below. Descend here. This is the beginning of a floodplain that will take you down to Burnhamthorpe Road Bridge. The path is broad and gravelled, and leads through a riverine landscape with crack willows and such.

The rapids here are caused by layers of shale, with few if any granite boulders, quite unlike the more easterly streams of the city. There are many accommodating places to sit down and chew, or watch, or doze on a warm afternoon.

When it appears, take the right fork, leading beneath the bridge. On the other side, climb the stairway to road level. This is the end of this walk.

GETTING BACK: Walk east along Burnhamthorpe Road to the 50 bus, which goes to the Islington Subway Station. If you left your car up at the Centennial Park entrance, take the subway back west to Kipling, take the 111 Kipling bus north to Eglinton Avenue, and transfer to the 32B westbound bus that will take you back to the beginning.

INTERLUDE 1
"IT'S ALIVE! IT'S ALIVE!"

Imagine yourself walking a downtown street early in the morning. There are interesting things to see: the different buildings, signs, window displays, long shadows and sharp contrasts. Certainly there's a variety of garbage blown about with each little puff of breeze. But as you walk, your mind wanders, because, well frankly, pretty quickly this cityscape becomes boring.

But then a car whizzes by. You hear the clatter of a garbage can being emptied up an alley. A cyclist whooshes along. A jogger crosses against a red light up ahead, with only a quick glance in both directions. The primary lifeforms are waking up—the city is becoming interesting. If you take this same attitude into the ravines with you, it quickly becomes apparent that while a knowledge of the geology is useful, it's the life there to which we, as sentient, curious beings, most strongly relate.

Come take a different imaginary trip, not into the city at dawn, but to a beaver pond towards the end of the day.

If you want to see the maximum amount of wildlife with the minimum of effort, visit a beaver pond. It's preferable that it be occupied, but that's not strictly necessary.

So there you are on a warm June evening, with the hope of meeting the builders. Of course, beaver are mainly nocturnal animals, but they often start their day well before sunset and continue until after sunrise. Many birds and animals remain quiet during the day, becoming active again later as the day cools. Consequently, the day and night shifts often overlap around sundown.

Everybody seems to enjoy a little drink at the end of the day, and the pond dwellers don't mind visitors dropping by. The resident ducks and Canada geese go on happily burbling to themselves, with the occasional *honk-honk* for variety. The grey tree frogs and their green cousins take a break occasionally, leaving a welcome silence.

A mink stops to take a look at you from across the way, before undulating off about his business. The fox and raccoon will be along later, when hunting's better. Every bird from a mile around seems to have come for its dip and sip, before retiring for the evening.

Finally, as the shadows lengthen and the pink sky is reflected in the leaf-dotted water, from the other end of the pond comes a loud *ker-plonk*. The beaver are out.

Often, though not always, gender equates with size—the male being the larger of a pair. But with beaver you can't always be sure that the largest is the male, as it would probably be in other species. However, you can usually assume that dad will be the first on the scene.

He may not have seen it all before, but he certainly has seen people. Mildly interesting, but as long as they mind their manners, nothing to get too excited about. He'll swim by with one eye pointed your way, nose and ears lifted above the water, make a turn, come back, make one more turn and swim on about his beaver business. Beaver eyesight isn't the greatest, but their senses of smell and hearing are first-rate. If the breeze blows towards you and away from him, and if you stop all movement except breathing, there'll be nothing to alarm him.

A few moments later along comes mom. She's an animal of decidedly different temperament. She may swim up in front of you and stop dead still. She'll glare at you with both eyes, sniff, sniff again and then *ker-plonk*, under she goes!

Surfacing a few yards away, she glares again, and again, *ker-plonk*. Then, just so there's absolutely no mistaking her intent, she'll follow up with a couple more *ker-plonks*, before swimming off in another direction.

Finally, along come the kids. They swim by, then come back and stop. They swim away and return, passing closer and closer, stopping, then closer still. Eventually even their curiosity is satisfied, and they'll leave in search of pond lilies or young green shoots. After all, their day is just beginning, and they need breakfast.

By now a bit of a moon is shining. Enough that, aided by the afterglow, you can see to pick your away across the top of the dam with fairly dry feet.

In the valley beyond, with your eyes focussed downward to avoid tripping, you might feel rather than hear the *whhhhhh* sound a large owl makes as it glides overhead. If you look up in time you'll see a big, dark shadow briefly obscure the moon. Before you reach the car or the bus stop, a passing train sounds its whistle. This prompts a chorus of yips from old and young at the coyote den a mile away.

Beaver are big brown rodents that cut down trees, build dams and slap the water with their tails (*ker-plonk*). All true, but there is more.

Beaver can trace their family tree back to a time before the sabre-toothed tiger and the mastodon. At that time they might grow to weigh 300 kilograms, about the size of a big black bear. You're most unlikely to see any of the beaver described by various European authorities in the eighteenth century. You'll miss the ones with monkey's hands, duck's feet, teeth curved to better hook fish and a tail that is

both a rudder and a building tool. Gone also are the beaver lodges in their former glory. They must have been something to behold. They were reported to be three stories high, built from fitted and notched logs, with each floor divided into rooms. The view from their windows and balconies out across the pond brought ease to the weary builder at the end of a hard day's labour.

Coincidentally, at the same time as Europeans were extolling the wonders of this rodent, they were well on the way to exterminating them in North America, as they already had back home in Europe. Had it not been for the invention of mechanized felt-making and a change in fashion in the mid-to-late 1800s, the beaver would have followed the passenger pigeon into oblivion. It took extensive lobbying in all jurisdictions to control beaver trapping in the early part of this century. This was followed by intense restocking efforts, until a degree of balance has been reached today, with some trapping and lots of beaver dams.

Though our modern animals don't match the reported wonders of their ancestors, they are nevertheless quite astounding in their own quiet way. In many places, especially where the land is less than fertile, the beaver and their ponds have a major role in shaping the environment and affect just about everything living in the area, plant and animal.

It all begins when young beaver leave home, pair up and go looking for a home site. They wander around, avoiding other established ponds, until they find a valley with a stream running through it. There have to be lots of trees, preferably including some aspen, and a place where the valley sides close in, creating a narrowing. An island or two would help. The idea is that they don't want to build any more dams than they have to, because they're hard to build in the first place, and they consume a lot of time in maintenance.

Why then, if it takes so much time and energy, build a dam at all? There's one common reason that any organism does anything—to be better able to survive and reproduce.

Like so many amazing phenomena, beaver-dam building is quite a simple process in essence. Directions for dam building would go something like this. Just grab a stick and shove it in the mud, then another close by, and so on. Then you scoop up some mud and pack it in the holes. Pile on a few more sticks, pat down some mud, and keep going till the water stops flowing over the top. Some of the "sticks" would qualify as fully grown trees by anyone's definition.

Beaver dig up mud from the bottom of the pond and carry it in their forepaws, propelling themselves with their hind legs. The dam needs to be more than a metre high to be deep enough to maintain a layer of unfrozen water at the bottom in winter, so the beaver can reach their food cache. A pair of beaver can build a dam

6 to 9 metres long in three or four nights. The longest dam recorded measured 1,200 metres. They're quite solid enough for a person to walk on, and there are tales of very old dams able to support a horse and wagon.

The process of lodge building begins in the same way as the dam, only it's centred on one spot rather than on a line between high points. You start with a pile of mud, then pile on sticks and slap on mud until there's a good big pile extending well above water level. Just be sure that the mud doesn't fill in all the spaces in the centre—you'll need some way for air to percolate in and out. Then you swim down to the bottom of the pond. First gnaw out a tunnel into the pile, then dig out a hole extending up above water level. To finish off, you excavate a couple of platforms, a small one at the end of the tunnels to stand on while you dry off and perhaps nibble some alder bark, and then a second, a metre or so in diameter, to sleep on. And there you are: home sweet home. You might also want to create a back-door tunnel, just in case a quick exit is ever needed.

Well, there's your basic beaver habitat, except for one thing. Lots of saplings and even some good-sized trees have been cut down for building purposes, and in the fall more will be taken for food. They're stuck into the mud near the lodge entrance, and the beaver snack on their tender inner bark during the winter. But usually there are lots more trees standing. As the water rises, their roots are covered, the soil becomes saturated, and there's not enough available nitrogen and oxygen left to keep them alive. So they die. And that is why most beaver dams are littered with dead trees, both lying in the water and still standing.

And life goes on. Little beaver grow up and produce more little beaver, and life of all kinds thrives on the pond. Only the trees seem to suffer. Beaver grow faster than trees, and that dam needs constant maintenance as the power of moving water works relentlessly to undo the beaver's work. The line of trees surrounding the pond withdraws slowly, year after year, until all that remains is a widening circle of scrub and brush. The beaver clear paths and dig canals to float trees down to the pond, sometimes even constructing a series of dams up a hill, following a stream, to float down some desirable alders. If the brush is thick and impenetrable, even for beaver, and if the soil conditions allow, they may build "plunge holes," which are holes with a long water-filled tunnel leading back to the pond. But in time they can do no more: the trees are just too far away.

A number of bad things can happen to the beaver. If home is close to a municipality or a road, they may be live-trapped and moved, or they may be dead-trapped for their fur. They may become food for predators. But if they stay alive long enough, when the trees have been cleared too far away from the pond, they may be forced to move on.

One way or another, eventually the pond is vacated, the dam or dams deteriorate, and the water level drops.

As it drops, the retreating water reveals a secret. In all the years that the pond has been there, the stream that feeds it has continued to carry sediment into it. The running water has collected sediment all the way from the stream's source, in runoff from rain and melting snow and ice. At the dam, the flow slows drastically, sometimes stopping altogether, and the particles the stream has been carrying have slowly dropped down to the bottom. Over the years, that bottom has slowly risen, and now that the water is leaving, a wide, flat, nutrient-rich field is revealed. In some locations, the new land is richer and more fertile than any other for kilometres around. This is what is called a beaver meadow.

Back to the beaver themselves and that tail-slapping habit. It doesn't sound like a slap; it sounds more as if someone has thrown a good-sized boulder into the water. They do use it to signal danger, but they also seem to use it conversationally.

As tails go, the beaver's is unusual. It's flat, about 30 centimetres long, and covered with leathery scales. (During the eighteenth century, bishops in Paris decided that the beaver's tail was not flesh, it was fish, so eating it during Lent and on fast days was okay.) It's mostly filled with fat, which helps in winter when food is scarce, and the animals use it as a prop to stay upright when gnawing down trees. It's not used in dam building, but you might see a wee little beaver being ferried across the pond on it.

If you see a small beaver that doesn't slap its tail, you're probably watching a muskrat.

CHAPTER 2

THE MIMICO CREEK
WATERSHED

Mimico Creek is described in some places as forming part of the eastern boundary of the Etobicoke Watershed, and in others as part of the western boundary of the Humber Watershed. It's sort of like trying to find out who you are by defining who you're not. (Can't be more Canadian than that!) It must be a watershed, or there would be no creek, right? But added to the evidence of our own eyes today, there's some history, too.

The First Peoples had a word for the area, recorded on an early map of Etobicoke Township as the Lamabineconce River. From this, somehow, were derived "Macaco," and "Omimeca," among others. Eventually the English settlers found "Mimico" the easiest to pronounce.

That original name meant, approximately, "Place of the Wild Pigeons," referring to what we now know as passenger pigeons. The area around the creek, with its mixed hardwood and evergreen forests, was one of two favoured nesting sites of the bird in the Toronto area. The other was east of Aurora. It was also a favourite stopover for others migrating south from the Bruce Peninsula.

We're not talking here about just a few birds roosting in a steeple. A century and a half ago there were literally billions of pigeons leaving their winter homes in southern hardwood forests to darken the skies for days as they made their way north. The nests were so thick in the trees that their weight would break off limbs. A flock of these pigeons settling in a farmer's newly sown field could, and did, make it barren within the space of an hour.

On the other hand, the First Peoples and many of the early settlers survived the freezing winters by eating from barrels of pickled pigeon and stores of smoked salmon. The birds were so thick on the ground, and in the air, that a person could go out with a long stick and kill enough to fill a barrel in a few minutes. And there's also another rather bizarre method reported. The pigeons favoured hickory trees for roosting, so all enterprising settlers had to do, so the story goes, was set a hickory tree on fire, and they would end up with a hundred or so barbecued birds all ready for the pickle barrel. (The story doesn't explain why the birds didn't just fly away!) Anyway, it is an often-recorded fact that wild pigeons sold cheaply in Toronto's farmers' market for most of a century.

Like Canada's "boundless" forests and "limitless" supplies of fish, the pigeons finally began to decrease in number, and by the late 1800s they were all gone. The last known passenger pigeon died on September 1, 1944, in the Cincinnati Zoo.

Humans hunting for food certainly hastened the demise of the species, but probably equally influential, if not more so, was the destruction of the birds' habitat, as forests were used to build more towns, which held more people, which killed more birds, and so on.

Although it doesn't look possible today, there was a sawmill on the creek, built by one John William Gamble, a native-born Canadian. It was located near the present CNR bridge. Gamble made his home close by the mill, and workmen built some huts for themselves down near the lake. Thus was founded the village of Mimico. There's a mid-century description of the place from *Smith's Canadian Gazetteer* of 1846:

> Mimico. A Village in the township of Etobicoke situate on Dundas Street, on the Etobicoke Creek [sic], nine miles and a half from Toronto. It contains about 150 inhabitants. A neat Wesleyan chapel is erected, and an Episcopal church is in the process of erection.
>
> Mimico contains two saw mills, one store, one physician and surgeon, two taverns, one blacksmith, one butcher, two shoemakers, two wheelwrights and wagon makers, two carpenters and joiners, one tailor.

About as typical a Canadian village of the time as could be imagined. One of the taverns was owned by one Thomas Montgomery. Due to its good solid stone construction and a lot of effort recently by people in the area, it is preserved to this day on the southeast corner of Dundas Street and Islington Avenue.

Mr. Montgomery was an Irishman, both by birth and by nature, and his biography is both entertaining and informative. He was, it appears, a man of strong will and moderate education, not uncommon for someone in his business in those days. He appears to have been involved in court proceedings more often than many others of the time, both as plaintiff and as accused. There is one incident of a fire of a competing tavern, involving hand-written warnings identified as originating from Montgomery, yet he was not convicted of arson as charged. One might speculate that he was not the type of individual that a local jury member would want to make an enemy of.

Considering the original owner's apparent character, it's ironic that today at Montgomery's Inn, in addition to taking a guided tour, we can also take our leisure and be served a nice cup of tea on weekday afternoons.

In the 1940s, during the Second World War, Etobicoke Township had the creek valley near the lake bulldozed flat to create industrial sites. And a polluting fuel spill a few years ago at Pearson International Airport once again focussed local attention on Mimico Creek. There is now a group of local people taking steps to begin the long process of bringing back some of the original form and beauty of the stream.

Today the stream runs through industrial land or behind backyards, and the narrowness of the valley precludes many country walks, so there's only one trail described here.

MIMICO WALK 1
MIMICO

DISTANCE: 2.5 kilometres, plus 1 kilometre to a bus on weekends

NOTE 1: Although it's relatively short, you should not undertake this walk when the ground is wet: there are some places where the trail can be very slippery, and it angles sharply down to the creek. When the water is high, the creek can be very fast between vertical banks, and a slip could have serious consequences.

NOTE 2: The Number 2 bus along Rathburn Road runs weekdays only. On weekends and holidays the nearest bus is about a kilometre away at either East Mall or Kipling. There's a footbridge near the end of the walk, allowing a return up the other paved side, for a fast trip back to the beginning.

GETTING THERE BY PUBLIC TRANSPORT: From the Kipling Subway Station at the west end of the Bloor/Danforth Subway line, take the 111 East Mall bus north to Eglinton Avenue.

GETTING THERE BY AUTOMOBILE: There is no public parking available in the start area. It's easiest to park at the Kipling Station parking lot and take the 111 East Mall bus north to Eglinton.

SUMMARY: Along the east side from Eglinton Avenue to Rathburn Road, the walk is along trails varying in style from promenade to slippery scramble. It's short but interesting.

THE WALK: Mimico Creek flows to the right, east from the bus stop. Go to the near side of the creek and turn right down the embankment to the end of a line of fence, the beginning of the trail. It can be partly overgrown in the summer, but it's used often enough to remain visible.

The creek here runs at the bottom of two concrete embankments. Watch your step along this stretch, especially in winter, because once on that concrete it can be very hard to stop sliding down into the creek. The water can be moderately deep and very fast after a rain, or when swollen by melted snow.

The trail runs close to the top of the concrete spillway, fortunately not too far. The space to the right between the creek and the road is open. After a little dip in the trail through a mini-ravine, you'll enter a treed area.

In many places the trail follows right along the edge of the creek; it's further back in others. The creek loses altitude precipitously along here, resulting in many little riffles, rapids and waterfalls.

There are a number of storm sewer outlets along this part of the creek—it's not only the Don that suffers from having storm runoff suddenly dumped into it from time to time.

The winter form of the creek might be described as "efficient," with its vertical banks, depth, and goodly speed, and woe betide the child or dog who falls into it.

In the summer, though, the creek meanders lazily down here, gurgling over pebbles and little rapids. Considerations of pollution aside for the moment, it's a thoroughly pleasant place for children or adults to dip their feet or wade around in. What a difference a few centimetres of rain or melted snow can make!

When the trail forks, stay to the left. Further on, a sidewalk comes down from the right and crosses the creek via a footbridge.

The path begins to get somewhat hairy along here: this is one of the sections that can become downright dangerous in wet weather. The old riverbank has moved in quite close, and at first you follow the very edge of the creek. Begin edging up the side of the old bank—someone has attempted to make it safer by driving in stakes to support some fallen limbs along the outside edge. They are a great help until you reach the ones that have rotted away. The problem then is finding trees or roots to grab, or to use for a foot stop. This stretch provides good healthy exercise in dry weather.

A spur of land runs down to the creek. Great chunks of old sidewalk have been tossed down its sides, probably to limit erosion, but they certainly make walking and climbing difficult.

At the top there's a little piece of mown grass, and on the other side a stream pours in from the right. Just follow it back a few yards to the outlet portal, walk behind it and follow the trail back down the other side. Curve right to walk along beside the creek again. At the next fork in the trail, stick to the left.

Sometimes the only wildlife you'll see on a walk is dead. It's probably the only way you'll get to see the night creatures like mice and moles. Just don't get too close: wild animals are infested with all sorts of little things inside and out, some of which would be quite eager to switch allegiance from their dead host to a living human. A few can be very nasty. Keep your head and face at least a foot away from any body, and use a stick to poke or move it, if desired.

Some people like to take home a memento. Best get some expert advice from a book or other source before bringing something into your living room you might regret later. It's amazing what a fallen bird's nest can introduce into your life. You could be scratching for days.

Continue on past a wide mown swath coming downhill from the park above and a long series of steps coming down from the right as well. The trail angles off to the right into a woods. At the forks continue straight ahead. There's a section containing a number of trails between here and the old riverbank on the right. Feel free to explore.

After crossing a streamlet, there's a bit of a scramble up the other side and across the top of some gabion baskets.

At the bridge at Martin Grove, when the trail forks, continue on down under the bridge. Continue to follow the curve around towards the Rathburn Road Bridge and take the fork up to the right to the road.

If you wish, you can cross the bridge and go back the way you've come, following the paved path upstream on the east side of the creek. Look out for bicycles.

GETTING BACK: During the week, turn right, and cross the road to a bus stop at the corner of Martin Grove and Rathburn where you can catch the Number 2 bus to Kipling Station. On the weekend, you'll either have to retrace your steps or walk about a kilometre either west or east to the East Mall or Kipling. All buses seem to lead to Kipling from here.

GULLS

They're often called seagulls. But even though found around the oceans of the world, they're as likely to be seen following the plough or sitting outside a fast-food joint in the middle of the continent. They're not even, strictly speaking, sea birds. Birds that live pretty much exclusively on the oceans ingest a lot of salt water, and if they didn't get rid of the salt somehow, it would kill them in short order. All birds have glands to excrete salt, but in sea birds they are highly developed: they look like oversized nostrils high up on the bill. Gulls' are relatively undeveloped, so they need fresh water to drink in order to survive.

The gulls of Toronto have a mixed history. Presumably they have ranged the Great Lakes since the last glacial retreat. Certainly they were well established when European settlers arrived. The first decline in their numbers became noticeable in the 1850s, as the creation and expansion of the waterfronts not only of Toronto, but towns all along the north shore of Lake Ontario began to cut into breeding grounds. Then a few years later came the plume trade, or from the birds' point of view, the plume wars.

Some individuals had always used bird feathers to add beauty and marks of privilege to themselves. Warriors with feathered headdresses and Incas with feathered capes had used these sexual attractants from male birds since time immemorial. But since there were few really important people at any given time, the bird populations were never seriously affected. With the dawn of democracy in Europe and North America, however, everybody became important, and anyone who could afford a feather or two could wear them.

So milliners put a feather on their creations. Then a few feathers, then a wing, then the whole bird, then a couple of birds. In an orgy of excess, even eggs and nests were incorporated into madam's chapeau. There were many thousands of women who could afford a few feathers, so the demand exploded. Anything that could fly was in danger. Whole colonies were wiped out, and egrets and some other species were in danger of extinction. It wasn't until after the turn of the century that a movement led by members of the Audubon Society to take the birds off the ladies' hats began to gather momentum. Books were written, pamphlets distributed and meetings held to decry the destruction of avian species. But it wasn't until after the First World War that the practice finally ended.

Gulls with their pure white and dove grey plumage didn't fare better than any other species. By the end of the first decade of the century the ring-billed gull had all but disappeared as a breeding species from the Great Lakes.

Slowly, slowly the numbers recovered, but by 1960 there were still fewer than 60,000 ring-bills in all the Great Lakes, mostly around Georgian Bay.

Then came the Leslie Street Spit.

After the end of the Second World War, the volume of shipping in the Great Lakes bound for the heart of the continent increased considerably. When the Canadian and American governments created the St. Lawrence Seaway, Toronto, along with some other cities on the Great Lakes, became a bona fide seaport.

But our little harbour and small slips and off-loading facilities weren't up to the job, so it was decided to build a new, modern and larger outer harbour. This would not only assure the city's place as a major seaport, it would also provide a place to dump all the earth dug up from the basements of a rapidly expanding city, and all the broken pavement and walls and partitions from the old structures being demolished to make way for the new. So the parade of dump trucks down to the foot of Leslie Street began, and continues to this day.

Then someone came up with the bright idea of making a big steel box and putting the small shipments in that, so they could be easily loaded on any ship. At the other end they would be offloaded onto a truck or train, and taken anywhere on the continent. The idea caught on and soon shipbuilders created vessels just to carry these containers. From the shippers' point of view, rather than spending extra weeks and all the extra costs incurred navigating up the seaway and into the lakes, why not just offload at Halifax, put the containers on trucks, and use the existing road system to get them inland.

There went the reason for Toronto's outer harbour. But the idea had developed a momentum. The trucks kept coming and dumping, and the new jut of land kept growing. And so was born the Leslie Street Spit. Many years later it was renamed Tommy Thompson Park, after a former Toronto parks commissioner who had done more than any other individual to preserve Toronto's parks and ravines.

So here was this long stretch of sand and gravel and old concrete light standards, just a metre or so above lake level. A favourite nest site for gulls is a sand and gravel beach, with or without concrete light standards, beside or in the middle of a body of water. Guess what happened.

As mentioned, in 1960 there were fewer than 60,000 ring-billed gulls, the most common variety by far in the Great Lakes. In 1973 there were only 21 nests

at Toronto's eastern headland of the outer harbour (the Leslie Street Spit). But by 1976 there were 10,000 nests, and by 1984 there were 74,500 nests. It is now, as it was then, one of the largest gull colonies in the world.

Panic, panic. The sky is falling! The gulls are taking over the world! They're killing all the songbirds, eating all the duck food, and soon they'll be snatching babies from their prams! The media a few years ago sold its wares, as it so often does now, by appealing to their readers' fears. What to do about the menace of Toronto's gulls. Fortunately, the solution was not left to media-fired public opinion, and a few professionals who actually knew something about the subject counselled calm.

The spit, Tommy Thompson Park, is now the nesting place for a great many gulls, terns, and cormorants, which had also mostly disappeared from this end of Lake Ontario. Recently black-capped night herons have moved in as well. In addition there are songbirds, muskrats, foxes, coyotes, rabbits and lots of other things. And all, all, without any human interference. The wind blew seeds, herbs and trees and bushes grew, and birds and animals found their ways to this new habitat.

The one thing most difficult for humans to master is the art of doing nothing. And in spite of constant pressure "to do something useful" with this unique spit of land, so far it's been allowed to be simply itself, and to allow the life of the world to establish itself in all its wondrous diversity.

What may be most attractive to us about gulls, along with the aesthetic appeal of their form and appearance, is their behaviour, at times so reminiscent of our own. The drive to be first, the never-ending arguments over who will get the choicest garbage, the strutting and preening, the distress of a lone bird away from the flock, possibly facing eventual death because of an injured leg or wing, all remind us of our own "unique" human foibles.

THE HUMBER
WATERSHED

Now the birchbark canoe was a wonder of lightness and strength, granted, but can you imagine toting one all the way from Lake Ontario, 50 kilometres up to the Holland River and the Holland Marsh, and then on to Lake Simcoe? That's what First Peoples and some French fur traders did in order to reach Georgian Bay. From the original Canadians' point of view, it avoided the long paddle down to the Trent system on Lake Ontario. That lake can throw up some big and dangerous waves from time to time. It also avoided the possibility of meeting marauding Iroquois. The French went because that's where the Canadians took them.

In the early days the river they used was called Toronto, and its valley formed the southern portion of what came to be known as the Toronto Carrying Place. As the name suggests, it was actually mostly one long portage to Lake Simcoe rather than a waterway. As you follow one of the trails described here along the east side of the main river, take a moment to look around, and imagine yourself as part of a group of people, sharing the weight of a large canoe or carrying a huge pack on the long, long trail north.

The first recorded European to travel the route, in 1615, was the French trader and explorer well known to those familiar with early Canadian history, Etienne Brulé. He was travelling with a party of Huron, his eventual destination being the Susquehanna River in the United States, where he hoped to enlist the locals into a war with the English. But that's another story.

The first known map of the route was drawn for Samuel de Champlain, governor of Quebec, in 1632. The pathway was so old then that in places it was worn 30 centimetres deep. This long, difficult trail later became famous, or infamous, with traders, explorers and missionaries.

By 1651, the Iroquois Confederacy had killed or driven out the tribes originally inhabiting the area, the Huron, the Neutrals and the Petun (names the French gave to the Original Peoples). This was not ethnic cleansing as we know it today, because all the tribes concerned were of the same cultural and linguistic group. No, it was just good business. The Iroquois wanted to control the very lucrative fur trade, and were eliminating competition. To maintain control of the territory, the Iroquois built fortified villages on both the Rouge and Humber

Rivers. The one on the Humber was called Teiaiagon, meaning "It crosses the river," referring to a nearby fording place. It was probably situated near what is today called Baby Point, a bend in the river north of Bloor Street.

First Peoples from the north and west were taking furs down the lake to the British in Oswego, so the French built a little fort and house on the east side of the river in 1749. It was so profitable during its three months of operation that they built a larger fort on the eastern edge of Humber Bay the next year. Actually, during the last half of the 1700s, the name "Toronto" referred more to this area than to that around the Don, explaining in part why Governor Simcoe called his settlement "York." Remember, he didn't much like local place names, preferring more "civilized" English ones. It was he who renamed the Toronto River the Humber.

One of the first things the good governor wanted to do after establishing York was build a road to the north to promote settlement. While casting about for a route, he was of course informed of the Toronto Carrying Place, and set out to follow where it might lead. Where it lead him was waist-deep into the Holland Marsh. After calming down and drying out he headed home, by a different route, and the Toronto Carrying Place was never mentioned again. He brushed himself off, pointed north and said, "Go that way!" And so Yonge Street was born.

The governor and his advisors decided that, if left to free enterprise, the provision of wood for the building of the new capital would be prohibitively expensive. So he had a sawmill built, to be known as the King's Mill. It was built at the first rapids of the Humber River, very close to where Bloor Street crosses today. They then hired an old soldier, formerly of His Majesty's Service, to operate it.

The soldier carried out the tradition of old soldiers since time immemorial: he managed to give the appearance of great activity without actually doing very

much. Nevertheless, some trees were felled, some lumber was cut, and the building of the new government offices went on apace, with the mill operator selling any lumber in excess of government needs for his own profit. This was part of the contract and all quite legal. But within a very few years the operator complained that the mill was falling apart, and everybody who visited agreed. Some said it was because the operator had not maintained it, others stated that a government strapped for cash had skimped badly on the original construction. Whatever the case, by the time the original lease was up the mill was virtually worthless, and government efforts to find new operators were eventually only marginally successful. The monster burned down in 1803, mercifully ending the fiasco. The whole thing ended up costing more than it was worth, and so began a tradition of government-sponsored projects that continues to this very day.

Mills sprang up wherever there was a sufficient drop in the river to power them. Grist mills were as important to the locals as sawmills, because they meant settlers could grind the grain they grew and feed themselves over winter. After about 1850 a number of woollen mills were also built. In 1846 there were sixteen grist mills, thirty-seven sawmills and six woollen mills, for a total of fifty-nine. Fourteen years later in 1860, there were twenty-four grist mills, fifty-six sawmills and eleven woollen mills, for a total of ninety-one. It should be remembered that these mills were spread out along the whole length of the river; however, there was still a whole lot of milling occurring on the lower Humber. And although steam-powered mills began to replace them, as late as 1914 there were still a number of water-powered mills on the river.

The most recent big change to hit the Humber was Hurricane Hazel in 1954. This event is covered in more detail in Interlude 6, but suffice it to say here that the structure of the Humber Valley as it appears today has much to do with the aftermath of that natural disaster, and the creation of the Metropolitan and Region Conservation Authority. Those of us who enjoy the valleys in their present forms can be grateful for the determination of the members of that authority to make the hard decisions that have kept buildings off the floodplain to this day.

While taking a break and enjoying a drink or snack in one of these valleys, take a moment to look around. Nothing will ever bring back the thousands of huge pines shipped off to make masts for the British navy. It will take persistence and determination to restructure the river so that salmon can once again return to the upper reaches to spawn.

None of the walks described is dangerous. All will provide pleasure and beauty. Enjoy.

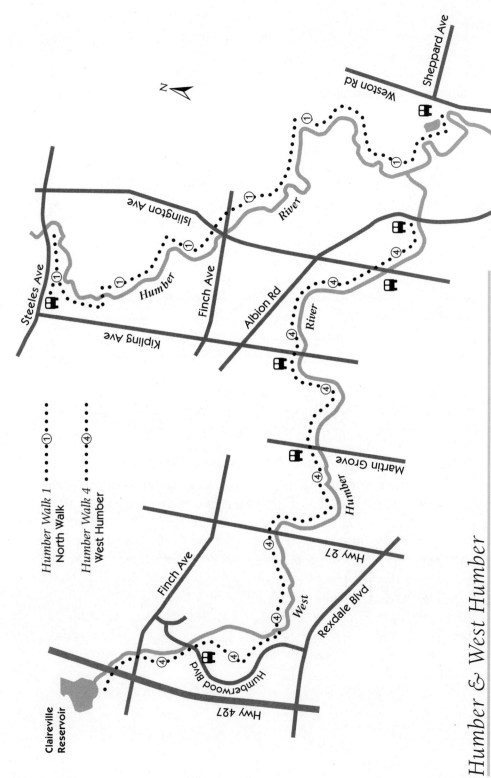

Humber Walk 1
North Walk

Humber Walk 4
West Humber

Clareville Reservoir

Clairville Reservoir

Humber & West Humber

34

Lower Humber River

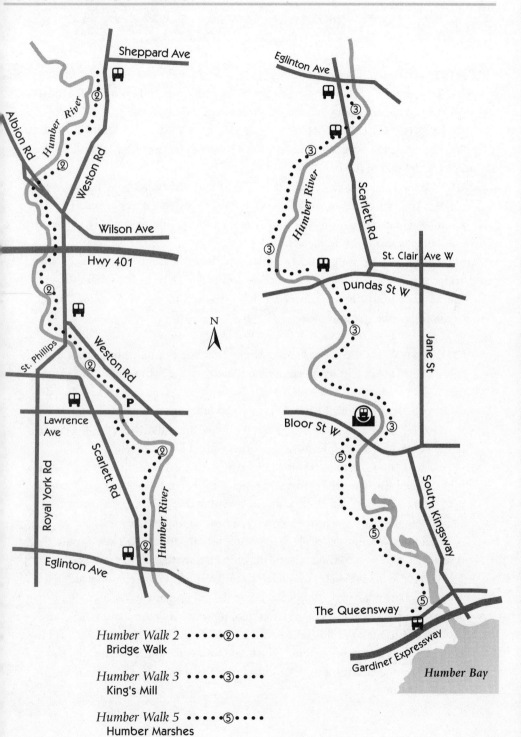

Sheppard Ave

Humber River

Albion Rd

Weston Rd

Wilson Ave

Hwy 401

St. Phillips

Weston Rd

P

Lawrence Ave

Scarlett Rd

Royal York Rd

Humber River

Eglinton Ave

N

Eglinton Ave

Humber River

Scarlett Rd

St. Clair Ave W

Dundas St W

Jane St

Bloor St W

South Kingsway

The Queensway

Gardiner Expressway

Humber Bay

Humber Walk 2 • • • •②• • • •
Bridge Walk

Humber Walk 3 • • • •③• • • •
King's Mill

Humber Walk 5 • • • •⑤• • • •
Humber Marshes

35

NORTH WALK

DISTANCE: 7.5 kilometres

NOTE: The walk follows paved paths, trails, near-trails and no-trails. It's mostly easy walking, and only one or two short boggy stretches.

GETTING THERE BY PUBLIC TRANSPORT: Take the Bloor/Danforth Subway Line to Kipling Station, then the 45 Kipling bus north to Steeles Avenue (almost the end of the line).

GETTING THERE BY AUTOMOBILE: There is no parking lot near Steeles. The secondary streets are residential, and some parking can usually be found. Alternatively, parking is available at the Kipling Subway Station and the 45 bus will take you north to Steeles.

SUMMARY: The walk follows a paved path south from Steeles to the first bridge across the Humber, then it follows trails for the most part along the east side of the Humber River, down to a point where it meets Weston Road, at the beginning of Sheppard Avenue.

THE WALK: Walk to the east along Steeles from Kipling, to the beginning of the guard rail on the bridge across the Humber River. To the right there's a gravel path descending to the river valley on a long, gentle slope. At riverbank level, the path turns to the right. Follow the trail as it curves to follow the river and climbs slowly.

Down by the river itself there's a little flat wetland that attracts a great blue heron every once in a while, as well as other water birds.

Further along, on the left side of the path, there's a row of spruce which some have dubbed the "candelabra trees." Some of them have twisted limbs, growing up a metre or more, jogging off to the side, and then continuing vertically.

Follow the path down from Kipling Avenue to the left, down across an old steel bridge spanning the river. Make a sharp right, following close beside the river's edge. When you come to a small wetland, scramble up to road level.

When the road veers off to the left towards a parking lot, continue along the verge. Soon the main path swings around to the left too, but there's a smaller path along the edge. Up ahead there's a wetland; in times of high water the level rises to cover the river end of this stretch, but for much of the year the land is soft but passable. If it's a high-water time, go left and follow the track around this patch; if not, continue straight ahead. In either case the two paths meet again on the bank on the other side.

Here there's a gigantic clump of willows consisting of about a dozen large trunks. This tendency of crack willows to grow in clumps is common in these riverine lands, but there aren't usually as many mature trees in one bunch as there are here. Trunks of 40 to 45 centimetres diameter are common in some trees.

When the trail forks, stay left, even though it means having to duck under a couple of trees and scramble over some others.

A bridge marks the meeting of Finch and Islington Avenues. Here, under the roadways, you can listen to the cooing of the rock doves. But when you move be careful where you step—they do more than coo.

The path runs parallel to Finch for a little way. Walk up towards the entrance from the street. Look to the right where there's a large section of newly planted growth, with a trail running along the left side. Follow the trail. If it's not immediately visible, have faith, there's a gully a bit further down, and you should be on the left side of it.

Take a sharp S-curve to the left, climb a small bank, and you'll emerge from the trees into a field. The trail forks: take the one to the left. The trail then rises a bit and intersects the path from the bridge. Follow the path to the left for a few yards, past a patch of staghorn sumac, to where it meets another along the river's edge, then stick to the river when the trail fades. Rejoin the path again when necessary—the river nestles in close beside it. Fickle as rivers are though, after a quick cuddle, it soon wanders off again, making a sharp right turn.

There's a trail along the edge, which is well defined through a stretch of horizontal trees and wild grape vines. In the winter, tracks on the ice can be especially clear, the dark ice contrasting with a light dusting of snow. Counting on the ice to support your weight while you take a closer look could be a mistake of the wet kind.

Turning to the left again into a meadow, the trail shows its age by its depth.

There's a little bridge over a stream, which the paved path crosses, and the trail follows the path. Follow the river along a ridge a few metres back from the edge.

Both trail and river twist back and forth through this wide grassland until they come to a footbridge that carries the paved path over the river yet again. Follow a different paved path angling off to the left towards a hydro right-of-way. There's a stream, too wide to step over, running beneath the power lines. The objective is to go upstream and find a fordable spot. When the path turns more left, over to the right there's a large school up on the hill, with a broad meadow stretching down to the creek. Walk towards it. Rocks have been tossed into the stream and, at most times, there are enough there to provide stepping stones for a dry passage.

Once across, walk straight ahead for a few yards, then take the trail running off to the right through the woods.

Back by the river again, the trail travels partway up the long, sloping bank. At the top of the bank turn sharp right and take the trail leading back down the hill. It's a little hard to see in some seasons, but there's a groove down the middle, making it easy to follow. A grove of young Manitoba maples stands to attention on the right, and just past them there's a trail beside the hydro lines.

The trail goes off to the right along with the river. Soon it moves away along a ditch, before swinging to the left, keeping in line with the river. Most of the trees lean strongly out towards it.

Make a sharp left to avoid the river. Keep turning left, back up beneath the hydro lines. Here a serious wetland bows in from the river; you can tell where it is by the trees lining the side and end.

Climb up, up, up the bank and at the top there's a trail along backyards. After you descend once again there's a field all planted in trees and shrubs. Cross beside the hydro lines.

On the other side, back in the woods, you may have to cast about for the trail, but it's there. A little further in, there's another of those small ditch-like valleys that occur in these lowlands from time to time. Turn left and follow it. On the right there's a huge, bulgy old willow tree.

Across the river now there's a stream that comes burbling in from the west. It's the West Humber River.

Both river and trail have their own agendas until a bank cuts across in front, and atop the bank there's a pond. Since you can choose to go either right or left, go right. This pond, when not frozen, is usually home to a flock of Canada geese. There are well-used playing fields on the east side of the pond, but on the west it's quiet most times, with lots of places to sit beside the water and watch.

The pond outlet flows into a culvert. Cross and continue on to the right towards the river. There's a wide path now along the river, both turning to the right up ahead. This walk continues straight up the bank leaving the paved path behind. At the top is Weston Road.

GETTING BACK: To find the TTC, turn left and walk up in front of St. Basil-the-Great College School, across from the end of Sheppard Avenue. There's a bus stop. Take the 165 bus to the Wilson Subway Station.

To return to the beginning of the walk, cross the street to the bus stop on the east side. Take the 165 bus north to Steeles Avenue, and the 60 bus west to Kipling. Keep the transfer. Take the 45 south to wherever your car is parked, or the Kipling Subway, whichever comes first.

BRIDGE WALK

DISTANCE: 8 kilometres

NOTE: The walk follows paved paths, trails and animal tracks. There is a stretch across a bank face that is difficult in any sort of slippery conditions, and there is another optional section along the top of a rock retaining wall: you should only attempt this in good weather, and then with care. An alternate route is provided for this stretch.

GETTING THERE BY PUBLIC TRANSPORT: Take the 84 bus from the Downsview Subway Station on the Spadina line, west to Weston Road, or the 165 Weston Road North bus, leaving from the upper level of the Wilson Station, to Weston Road and Sheppard.

GETTING THERE BY AUTOMOBILE: It's easiest to park at a subway station such as Wilson and then take public transport. There's off-street parking near the Sheppard Avenue and Weston Road intersection.

SUMMARY: Begins on a newly constructed path on the east side of the Humber, and follows mostly beside the river down beneath Albion Road and Highway 401. The next part of the walk is along a park path beside the Humber, to Lawrence Avenue. The final bit is along easy trails again.

THE WALK: Cross Weston Road at the traffic lights, turn left and walk almost to the next bus stop. On the right is a trail down through a gate in the chain-link fence, towards a paved path. This trail can be slippery under certain conditions. At the bottom, turn left along the pathway.

When the paved path crosses on its own bridge, ignore it and keep to this eastern bank, following trails that lead on beside the water.

The bank soon drops down to the river on about a 45-degree angle. This is one of the two trickiest stretches in this walk. Depending on how slippery the slope is, you can either head straight across to the other side (there's a narrow trail a few centimetres wide), or go up to the top and ease your way along, holding on to the chain-link fence that runs along the edge of a park. When the soil is hard and dry, the straight-ahead trail is safe and easy.

At the other end of this passage, you may have to scramble to get on the trail coming down from the top. Further down that trail, there's a small but deep little ravine, with sides about 2 metres high. It's easy to get down, but takes a bit of ingenuity to get up. Persist—it is possible

As the river curves to the left, the trail starts a gentle climb and meets a road coming down from above. After passing the end of the road, the path continues its left turn, widens, and provides easy walking through the woods.

Scramble down another steep bank, and soon you'll come upon a pair of bridges. Just before these, though, there's an ancient willow worth noting, with a trunk larger than 1.5 metres in diameter at the base. Some parts are dead, but there are also many that are very much alive and strong.

The southerly, newer, more heavily travelled bridge carries Albion Road across the river valley. After the bridges, the path testifies to its age by its depth.

The trail first follows beside the river, then tends away again, and in time it presents three forks. Let's do the Canadian thing and take the centre one, eh? The trail becomes obscure, but just keep going. It's actually been dug out a bit to make a good flat path with solid footing.

There are a couple of bridges here, the main one carrying Highway 401 itself, and a lesser one carrying an access ramp. The next bridge is a foot/bicycle crossing to the other side. Over there are a small park and the Weston Golf and Country Club.

Go up the bank at the bridge, and stay parallel to the river. It's easiest to just follow this path to where it curves to the left and becomes a street further inland.

At that point, there's an A option, B option situation. The A option is for summer, and for those who enjoy scrambling over rocks beside the river for a quarter of a mile. Option B is for winter and people who prefer to walk upright.

Option A: Continue along beside the river as it curves to the left. Just before you run into the bank, look downriver to the base of the railroad bridge pylons, where you should be able to see a shelf around their bases. If you can see the shelf, the water is low enough to allow passage, and you can continue. If not, take Option B. The shelf may look too narrow, but have faith, if you can see it, you'll be okay.

There's a storm sewer outlet coming out of the bank, so climb down this side, cross on some stone blocks, and up the other side. You can walk downstream on top of those big stone blocks at times, or step down a row or two onto their edges. Hold on to the bushes!

At the bridge, you'll see that the way around this pylon is on the shelf you looked for further back. Fortunately it's wider than it appeared from back there, and is easily traversed.

Once around, you'll be just about at river level most times of the year. Right in front of you is an outstanding (literally) example of Dundas shale. This is the rock foundation upon which much of Toronto is built, and here is a rare opportunity to come nose to nose with it. Pretty crumbly stuff, isn't it?

Stick to the trail that's closest to the river.

Just before the St. Phillips Street Bridge the trail becomes a wide path. On the other side of the bridge is the flight of steps that will carry those who have taken the B option down to this level.

Option B: Head for the road on the other side of the park; it's called Cardell Avenue. Follow it up the hill to Weston Road. Turn right and walk along Weston Road beneath the railway bridge to St. Phillips Road. Cross at the traffic lights, and turn right towards the bridge, then walk down the steps.

Proceeding beside the river, this wide, surfaced path will continue right on down to Lawrence Avenue.

It's possible to get down by the water almost any place along here and follow a trail along the water's edge. If you do that, there's a very good chance you'll be mobbed by mallard ducks, Canada geese, or both, looking to be fed.

There are rapids here and there along this stretch, and it's fun to watch the mallards shoot them. They're much better built for this sport than people are—they just draw their heads down into their feathers and scoot.

At the Lawrence Avenue Bridge there's an optional quitting point. To find a bus, walk out of the parking lot and turn left. Cross at the traffic light. Turn right and cross at the traffic light and you'll be on the south side of Lawrence Avenue. From here you can catch either the 52 or the 58 bus to Lawrence West Station on the Spadina Subway Line.

To continue the walk, cross Lawrence Avenue into the playground. Walk on through it, angling down towards the river, until you come to a path that crosses the river via a steel bridge.

On the other side, turn to the left and take one of the trails alongside the river. There are ups and downs, through woods and along the shore. Keep an eye open to your right, because up the bank a little there's a most unusual willow tree, so covered with bumps that one could be convinced that all willow trees should look like that. Follow along at your leisure down to Eglinton Avenue.

GETTING BACK: Cross to the south side and walk right. At the bus shelter you can catch the 32 Eglinton West bus to the Eglinton West Subway Station on the Spadina line. If you stay on this side, walk to the right to Scarlett Road and you can board the 29 Scarlett Road bus south to Runnymede Subway Station on the Bloor/Danforth Line. If you take the Scarlett Road bus, get a transfer. For those who drove, take the 32 bus east to Jane Street, then take the 35 bus north to Sheppard, and the 84 bus back west to Weston Road.

DISTANCE: 6.75 kilometres

NOTE: All of this route is easy walking. It follows either a smooth path or trails beside the river. There are no steep hills or really boggy patches.

GETTING THERE BY PUBLIC TRANSPORT: Take the Bloor/Danforth Subway to the Old Mill Station. Turn left outside along the fence to Bloor Street, left again to the bridge, and then down the steps and straight across the flood-plain to the river. Turn left.

GETTING THERE BY AUTOMOBILE: Take Bloor Street West to Old Mill Road (north side). From Old Mill Road, turn south on the west side of the bridge across the Humber into a parking lot, or turn north from the east side of the bridge into Etienne Brulé Park parking lot.

SUMMARY: From Bloor Street the trail follows the west bank of the Humber River, north to the Old Mill Bridge, crosses it and follows the river north through Etienne Brulé Park to just south of a railway bridge. It crosses the river again on a footbridge to Lambton Woods Park, then proceeds north on the west side of the river past Scarlett Road, to Eglinton Avenue.

THE WALK: At many times of the year, watch out for the fisher people. Watching them can be every bit as entertaining as watching birds. They can be seen tossing line for salmon, trout, suckers and carp. Many have strange little rituals, and occasionally there'll be a whole family of them calling back and forth to each other among the trees. Morning and evening are the best times to spot them, but in season there will be at least two or three in view at almost any time of the day. They frequent the riverside anywhere from the first weir up the river from here to well down towards the mouth. Serious watchers might want to keep notes; friends may not believe your stories without some kind of proof.

Anyway, keeping an eye out for cast bait, walk to the left, upstream beyond the subway bridge, keeping down beside the river most of the time.

The Old Mill Bridge is a quite lovely series of curved arches, built at a time when appearances counted for something. Cross the bridge on the left (north) side to Etienne Brulé Park, South Humber.

At the end of the parking lot lie the beginnings of two separate paths. One is paved and is labelled a Multiuse Trail. It's intended mainly for wheeled things such as bicycles and inline skates. The second is surfaced with bricks for a ways, gravel later, and is labelled Pedestrians. It's intended for walking people. Finally a park authority has recognized that people on bicycles and toddlers on tricycles cannot occupy the same space at the same time without someone, often both, getting hurt.

Early in some spring seasons, this whole floodplain may be filled with huge pans of ice more than 30 centimetres thick. As the ice breaks up and flows down river, it piles up against the bridge and backs up in this flatland, over to the base of the old riverbank. Look at the base of the trees along here and you'll see where the bark has been rubbed off in places, 30 to 60 centimetres above ground level. It wasn't beaver and it wasn't Boy Scouts; it was ice. The phenomenon is fascinating to watch and hear—from a distance.

On the right there's a stone washroom building, open in the warmer months. Take advantage of it now, as there's not a great deal of privacy along this walk.

The first of a number of weirs or dams across the river brings to mind the earlier statement about fisher persons, as this is where they are wont to gather in greatest numbers during the salmon run.

A few metres downstream of the weir there will be a line of them in full waders, spread across the breadth of the river, casting their lines up into the deeper water. Some will be sitting on the banks on both sides of the river, chatting and eating before returning to the fray. Every once in a while a line goes taut, a rod bends, and slowly, slowly the point where the line enters the water will begin to move. It may be up or down or sideways. It may be almost stationery for ten minutes at a stretch. Those who don't have a bent rod seem to ignore those who do, whether out of boredom, envy, or embarrassment is hard to say! Eventually the line moves downstream, and once in a while a huge fin will poke up above the rushing surface. Then the line may move back upriver, but nobody, neither fishers nor watchers, shows excitement, regardless of what happens.

Usually the strange dance of fisher and fish ends as the line and rod suddenly go slack. Now that the fish has been thoroughly exhausted, it goes back to trying to leap over this dam, which is just a bit too high. Eventually it will die, before having fulfilled its biological imperative to reproduce. The body will float back downriver until it washes up on a bank to feed raccoons and gulls.

The river is stocked with fingerlings from hatcheries, carried here in trucks and dumped. After years of feeding in the wastes of Lake Ontario, they return to the rivers and the cycle is ended.

The salmon that don't break the fishing line? They are edged slowly over to the shallows to be netted. Some females are milked for their roe, which, tied in little mesh bags, makes the preferred bait. Some are scooped out and taken home to be served to a hungry family, thereby providing them with a year's dioxin intake.

On the brighter side, there are rumoured to be plans afoot to cut a lower section into this one dam to allow some salmon upstream. There's passage around another dam upstream that may be negotiable, and it's possible that one day, with appropriate modifications to others, the fish will actually be able to find spawning grounds.

From this first weir there's a berm stretching across the plain, the outer end angled back upstream a little. The purpose is to keep in check future pileups of ice pans or flood debris.

There is a stretch now right beside the river hosting riverine growth and a serviceable little trail. Take that one.

Some tree trunks are wrapped with chicken wire, and the reason is visible close at hand. All along here there are mature willows partially girdled by beavers in years gone by. Those that were felled are long gone, of course. The beaver have returned a number of times over the years, and it's probable they'll be back again sometime. They may even be here now, lurking beneath the very bank you're standing on, or living in a hutch that looks like a pile of brush on some inaccessible part of the shore.

Above weir number three the floodplain widens out considerably and has been made into a regular park with trees and picnic tables spotted around. It's just as easy to follow the pedestrian trail along here, as the bank rises to about 3 metres in height and is steep.

At weir number four, there's playground equipment on the right—tennis courts, basketball hoops and a planting of young trees.

The sound of rapids announces weir number five. Just below it a concrete wall begins, so climb the bank to path level again.

Follow this on up to the bridge at Dundas Street West. The bicycle path goes up to the right to get over the road. The pedestrian path passes through a bright yellow cow-gate to cross beneath the bridge. Just beyond it, there's an old, deep trail heading down towards the river. That's ours.

The trail continues beside the water, up and down and through the occasional boggy bit. Up ahead, way ahead in fact, is an old railway bridge, supported by tall concrete pylons. Down below are more beaver-chewed stumps.

Just this side of the bridge there's a row of old bridge supports, currently holding up a green steel footbridge. This bridge is definitely designed for people; there's a wide spot with benches to sit on and enjoy the view up or downstream, and quite a view it is. It's reminiscent of engravings in travel books from the last century. At the other end, the bridge suddenly turns right when faced with a high bank of shale, and runs up beneath the railroad bridge where it meets a railed path coming down. The forest up ahead is Lambton Woods, the only real woodland on this walk, so let's enjoy it while it lasts.

One word of caution for winter walkers. None of these paths or trails is maintained in winter and, especially through here, ice forms from the passage of many feet. For those less nimble or with brittle bones, it may be best to walk beside the paths rather than on them.

The trail wanders through trees of many sizes and species, providing a great opportunity to dust off the old tree identification guide. It swings left, away from the river, but then makes a sudden right turn to a green wooden footbridge over a small, but deep and steep-sided ravine. Views up and down the stream are striking, including a bright trickle of water at the foot of miniature shale cliffs, and trees hanging out over the upper edges. Before the bridge was installed, crossing this stream was a real challenge.

You'll probably meet squirrels in here. On a quiet day in fall it's a little eerie to walk along and hear a rustling in the leaves behind. Turn slowly and you'll see half a dozen squirrels, sitting, staring, waiting. They expect to be fed. They don't intend to be intimidating. But that silent sitting, tiny bright black eyes, staring . . . .

Turn away, and the leaves rustle again.

You may see a group of birdfeeders in here, and some of the variety of birds they attract. One late January day in a warm winter you might see mourning doves, house sparrows, chickadees, purple finches, nuthatches, juncos, a downy woodpecker and a hairy woodpecker. Oh, and blue jays—you could hardly forget them. With luck you could also hear and see a couple of crows mobbing a Cooper's or sharp-shinned hawk. Possibly you might spot a lone robin or even a small flock; more are overwintering each year it seems. Add these to Canada geese, mallard and merganser ducks and ring-billed gulls you may have spotted down by the river, and it adds up to a good day for the casual birdwatcher.

Coming out of the woods, the pedestrian path leads up a hill past some huge juniper bushes. The top of this hill is owned by a small red squirrel. The parks department may believe it has jurisdiction, but anyone who comes here soon finds out who's in charge. He probably won't sit on your shoe, but he may be a few centimetres away, up on his hind legs giving you a beady-eyed stare. You should have brought food, and if you didn't, you should be afraid, very, very afraid. There are some black and grey squirrels around here twice his size, but they're no competition. Red squirrels are always aggressive, but they're often shy of humans. Not this one.

Further along, the path is separated from bicycles by a low fence and a line of bushes.

In this stretch of river valley, a number of outdoor interests have been accommodated, from the privately owned golf courses to the publicly owned, relatively unstructured woodlands, with bicycle and pedestrian pathways in between. There are even tennis courts. Having enough space makes a big difference, but providing several uses that don't interfere with one another is laudable.

At the Scarlett Road Bridge the path continues down underneath, with another of those hopelessly romantic signs, Cyclists Dismount and Walk. Very rarely! The path of discretion is up and across the roadway; the odds of being hit by a car are much less than those of encountering a bike zooming around a blind curve beneath the bridge.

It is possible to walk up to the left and catch a Scarlett Road bus. On the other hand it's only a short walk along the shore to Eglinton Avenue.

On the other side of Scarlett Road go right down across the paved path to the water. There are trails through here, but they sometimes fade away. Don't worry, just keep walking beside the river until the next one.

Close to the bridge is the first natural waterfall cum rapids to be seen on the river. There's a section of shelving shale dropping the water down a few centimetres with a satisfyingly chuckling little roar.

The bank begins to climb as the flat space disappears. Soon you're walking near the top of a wall of big stone blocks dropping 3 or more metres down to the river.

As the river makes a sharp turn to the right, you can see Eglinton Avenue up ahead. The path continues climbing around the turn, and soon it's running parallel to Scarlett Road to the end of the walk.

GETTING BACK: Crossing to the left you can catch the 32 Eglinton West bus to the Eglinton West Subway Station on the Spadina line. Cross Eglinton Avenue to the north and you can board the 29 Scarlett Road bus south to Runnymede Subway Station on the Bloor/Danforth line. If you take that one you'll need a transfer, or else you'll have to pay again to get into the Runnymede Subway Station. For those who drove, take the Bloor/Danforth Subway west back to Old Mill Station.

WEST HUMBER

DISTANCE: 9 kilometres

NOTE: Except for a slightly tricky stream crossing, a possible damp spot, and one short up-and-down bank scramble, this is all easy walking, mostly on clear trails and occasional paved paths.

GETTING THERE BY PUBLIC TRANSPORT: From the Finch Subway Station on the Yonge Street line, take the 36B bus west. Near the end of its route it crosses a bridge on Humberwood Boulevard, and there is a stop opposite the Humberwood Centre. That's where you want off.

GETTING THERE BY AUTOMOBILE: There is no public parking around here. There are, however, large parking lots near Finch and Albion Road, from which you can catch the 36B Finch bus west and proceed as above.

SUMMARY: The trail begins by skirting the Humber Arboretum, to the south of the West Humber River, crosses to the north side and follows its course to Albion Road.

THE WALK: After getting off the bus, cross to the east side of Humberwood Boulevard at the community centre, turn left, and go down to river level along the path beginning just before the bridge. You're now on the Metro West Trail, which follows the West Humber River all the way down to its confluence with the Humber. The walk will avoid this path when possible, but it will always be there for reference. It's a good path for wheels.

Option: (The following abbreviated description covers an optional side trip.) Turn to the left and walk upstream beneath the Humberwood Bridge. Continue on past the high stone retaining wall on the left, which is often overrun with wildflowers in the early summer. This stretch resembles an idyllic little English river, threading its way through clumps of cattails beneath overhanging trees. Continue on past the Highway 427 Bridge to the end of the paved path. Beyond here it's possible to follow trails up to the Claireville Dam. To enter the conservation area, follow the road left from the dam, and then right into the trailer park. From there, you're on your own.

Main Route: At the Humberwood Bridge turn right along the path to the footbridge, and the map showing the layout of the arboretum. Hanging below the map is a sign with an arrow pointing to the right, indicating the Humberwood Meadow Trail.

There's a well-defined trail up here, winding past the schoolyard and out across the flats among the trees. In winter you can follow the coyote or fox tracks through here; they know where they're going and gladly follow human paths as long as they're in the right direction. When the coyote's tracks lead beneath a limb that's only about half a metre off the ground, you've lost the main trail.

The trail meanders extensively, and there are a host of places to sit beside the river and watch the ripples or "pish" for birds. Pishing refers to the onomatopoeic noises birders make that mimic scolding calls, in order to attract birds to them. Of course, real bird lovers won't do this in breeding season, when parent birds are already over-stressed by the demands of feeding the bottomless maws of their young.

After crossing a healthy little stream 2 to 3 metres wide, the trail begins to ascend a long, gentle rise. At the top is the edge of a steep bank descending way, way down to the river.

At the fork, stay up here as a ridge walker. The one leading right often looks more used, but it leads away from the river.

At the next fork, take the path to the left, across the open space following the curve of the bank edge. Go down one hill and up the other to Humberwood Boulevard again.

After the rail ends you can move over to a trail along the bank edge; follow it while a berm builds up to the right. The path may be wide and clear in winter months but is almost totally hidden in summer.

Just before the trail drops off into a ravine, there's a path down to the left to a tennis court. Go first to the left following the tennis court fence, and then to the right around the end. Ease left and go down a gentle 3-metre drop to the flood-plain level. As the trail fades out, ease again over towards the river—you can find it by looking for the line of trees along the bank. The long-term objective is to get over beside it before meeting a stream coming down from the right, also marked by a line of trees. There's no rush, just choose left rather than right when there's an opportunity.

Incidentally, this broad browse-filled field has been known to attract deer. Don't be too surprised if some young buck suddenly bounds off, crashing and snorting, white tail flicking.

At the stream, head up the bank to the right for a bit to some willow trees growing in the stream bed. The debris caught around them provides a dry path to the other side.

Take the trail coming down from the right and cross the footbridge. On the other side, walk past the park bench to a trail into the forest. There's a sign low down indicating Riverside Trail. Turn sharp right to follow it as it winds over beside the river and then back through an arbour. When the trail dips right down beside the water, take care where you place your feet.

Continue past a footbridge on a paved path. College buildings are on the left, and further on there's a field, surrounded by a white painted steel fence. Follow this path towards the bridge carrying Highway 27 across the river.

Just before the bridge there's a sign reading Garfield Weston Garden Valley, and a bit past it another map of the Humber Arboretum. Follow the paved path under the left side of the bridge.

Follow the right fork of the path towards the river again. There's yet another footbridge up ahead; stay on this side.

The path goes off across the park. Keep the line of trees on the right and you'll soon come to a stream outlet marked by a fence along the top. Once past it, turn to the right and follow a trail along the verge between the mowed and natural grass areas, back towards the river. Over to the left there's an apple orchard, pink and glorious in spring, vinegary in the fall. There are many apple trees on this trail and they aren't sprayed.

At the Martin Grove Bridge, there's a path up the hill, so if you're tired, or the hour is getting late, climb up and get the 46 bus south to the Kipling Subway Station, or north to where you can transfer to the 73 Albion Road. It will take you back to the parking lot.

Just the other side of the bridge, there's a little stream emerging from beside it; it is easily stepped over. The path is deep and old. There are many beaver-nipped stumps from years past, pushing out new shoots to continue life. The part of a plant that shows above ground is only half the total individual, the roots down below being just as important to its life.

Follow the trail through the woods and along beside the river.

Just before the Kipling Bridge, there's a path up to the left towards the street, and again there's the option of catching a bus, the Number 45, north or south.

Follow the trail to a park with swings and slides at the far end. A long paved ramp gradually climbs the riverbank up to a set of wooden steps. You have a choice here. If the water is low, you can continue along the trail and cross a stream over stepping stones. There is a long waterfall here, rather spectacular in its own quiet way, as the stream tumbles down a long shale ladder, falling perhaps only a few centimetres at each step. The sight and sound are well worth a few minutes' time.

If you believe the water's too high, climb the ramp to the stairs. They will take you the last little bit up to street level. Walk up Lightwood Drive to an unnamed lane to the right. At the end of that take the steps down to the sidewalk along Albion Road. Walk to the right to the other side of the ravine, and turn right again. Follow the trail down beside the ravine. The trail swings slowly left to parallel the river, running along the top of the old bank. At the fence, there's a trail around the right end. It continues along the bank edge and then splits. Take the right branch down the bank to a lower level.

You'll come to a path partway up the hillside. For those with the time and inclination, it will be rewarding to follow this trail back to where that stream enters it. The path is clear.

Along the top of the bank on this side there are white pines. There have been few if any evergreens along this walk so far. Contrast the variety of species of trees in this valley with those in say, Highland Creek, and you'll see the difference between the Carolinian Forest Region to the southwest, and the Great Lakes–St. Lawrence Mixed Forest to the east and north. Some say the dividing line is in High Park, although there is of course much overlap.

Next on the agenda is the Islington Bridge.

Past the bridge, the trail leads up the hill. There's a street coming down here making an acute-angled turn just ahead, not far from the bank, with houses all along both sides. Stick to the bank, past the yellow traffic barrier, alongside the brick house, to a place where you can, with the aid of shrubs and roots, clamber down to the river's edge. Caution and care are needed in equal measure to keep dry feet, but it's only a short distance to a place beyond the backyard where you can pull yourself up the bank again. It would be helpful if someone would drop a load of rock in here.

The trail, wide here and well used, is back on a flat stretch travelling along parallel to, but away from the river

The left bank closes in again as the trail rises somewhat. As you approach the Albion Road Bridge and the end of this walk, keep close to the bank, so that just where the bridge begins you can step over a fence onto the sidewalk.

It's possible to cross the road, cross the bridge, and follow the stream down to the Humber, but this guide ends here.

GETTING BACK: Turn left to the bus stop where you can catch the 73 Royal York bus going to the Royal York Subway Station on the Bloor/Danforth line.

For those who drove, cross Albion Road and catch the 73 northbound bus that will take you back to Finch Avenue and the parking lot.

HUMBER MARSHES

DISTANCE: 5.5 kilometres

NOTE: Up and down one steep hill and a couple of shorter ones. Most of the rest is flat walking on paved path, trails and city streets. The trail often overlaps one of Toronto's new Discovery Walks, but side trips make it something quite different.

GETTING THERE BY PUBLIC TRANSPORT: Take the Bloor/Danforth Subway to Old Mill Station. Go left from the station to Bloor and then to the bridge. Just before the bridge, take the stairs down on the left side and go to the roadway below.

GETTING THERE BY AUTOMOBILE: Take Bloor Street West to Old Mill Road (north side). From Old Mill Road, turn south on the west side of the bridge across the Humber into a parking lot.

SUMMARY: The walk begins at the Bloor Street Bridge and goes south, out and back along a stretch of land running between the river and a slough. The trail then follows along the river past the Toronto Humber Yacht Club to urban streets, where a second loop explores a marshy area. After continuing along urban streets again, the trail follows the river to Queen Street.

THE WALK: Begin walking towards the river, but before reaching the last bridge support, ease over to the right, crossing beneath the bridge, and continue to the river's edge; it's steep and about 2 metres high here. This section of river, down to Lake Ontario, is broad and slower than sections further north, with marshlands on both sides.

This walk will be especially attractive to anyone looking for waterbirds. In places, both Canada geese and mallard ducks nest regularly, and there are year-round flocks of both. There is also beginning to be a small, year-round population of mute swans frequenting this river, Grenadier Pond, Tommy Thompson Park, and other locations on the waterfront. In migration season, mostly May and September, a dramatic variety of birds large and small use this valley as a flyway to summer nesting or winter retreat grounds.

The trail winds around a bit, but keeps mostly to the bank edge.

In time you'll come face to face with a steep, high bank rising out of what appears to be a stream. There's a path along beside it leading into the crack willow growth. Here there are a number of trails; choose as you wish—they all come to the same good end.

Other than raccoons and squirrels, there's not usually a great deal of wild animal life or tracks down here. The action is all on the water and in the air.

The "stream" is soon revealed to be the other end of the slough you started from, and the trail returns to the Bloor Street Bridge. Once there, turn left around the end of the slough to the roadway. Walk south along the roadway for a while, leaving behind Bloor Street, the subway and the looming apartment buildings. When the road curves right, keep on straight ahead, along a path across a field.

On the other side, climb the hill to the roadway.

Walk beside a log rail along the left side of the road. It goes up to the left and follows the edge of the long steep bank that falls away to the river below. There's a most expansive view from up here, all across and along the Humber and down to the slough behind the riverbank on the other side.

When the road curves off to the right, continue straight ahead to an abrupt right turn. The Toronto Humber Yacht Club is directly down to the left. Soon you'll have to descend a steep little hill back down to the road. At the bottom, follow the trail across the field and head to the left towards a parking lot. Take the road up the old riverbank to the top.

Walk along a street, turn left onto Riverwood Parkway and then left again on Stephen Drive. Walk to the end at the black-and-yellow checkerboard sign. There's a trail down to the right. It's quite steep and can be treacherous in slippery weather.

At the bottom you can bear witness to the carnage that hungry beaver can inflict on a forest.

Walk out along the finger of land that hooks to the right along the path of the river, leaving a long, shallow pond inside on the right. At the end of the finger, turn right again, to a forest of purple loosestrife. It often exceeds 2 metres in height, purple-flowered in summer, brown and sturdy in winter. Follow the inner edge of the slough back to the bank and scramble back up the hill to Stephen Drive.

Walk along the street, past Berry Road, to the point where the paved path curves off to the left beside a South Humber Park sign, diving back down towards the river valley.

Just before the path crosses a culvert and stream, go left along a trail. It skirts the trees to another trail running across it. Go up to the left, and at the fork make a sharp right turn and follow along beside a row of cedar trees.

At the river again, turn to the right along the bank, to a short, sharp, slope down to the flats. Take the trail to the right, travelling along partway up the hill. You may have to step over some fallen trees, and in time you'll find a passage down to the left into the valley. Cross a little stream and climb the other side.

Back at park level, lo and behold, there's a washroom, open only in warm months. At any time of the year, the unique shape of the roof in front of the washroom has peculiar acoustic qualities. Give it a try—stand in the middle and clap.

Follow along beside the trees marking the edge of a bank, eventually descending back beside the river. Here at backwater level, willow trees grow along the edge, and you can follow along the flats for a way. The willow demonstrates one of its unique abilities along here. If the water level rises, the willow puts out roots to take advantage of it. Consequently, in low-water time, the lower trunk looks bearded.

You'll be forced back up towards the paved path, just past where it meets a high concrete wall. This is the eastern boundary of a sewage disposal plant. Most times its function is not apparent, but sometimes, when conditions are ripe and the wind is from the west . . . .

Moving along smartly, there's a long row of pussy willows, which have been pollarded so that each spring there will be a crop of new stalks sprouting their unique catkins.

From here it's easiest to follow along the paved path towards the roadway. Just before the bridge, take the right fork, ramping up to street level. Follow along the street until you come opposite the place where the streetcar tracks turn left. Cross the street and, with care, walk along beside the tracks until you come to the eastbound sign post.

GETTING BACK: You can get on the eastbound Queen streetcar to Yonge Street Subway, or transfer to the 504 Roncesvales streetcar to the Dundas West Subway. For drivers, the same, but take the subway to the Old Mill Subway Station, turn left and left again, and go down the steps beside the Bloor Street Bridge to the parking lot below.

INTERLUDE 3
RAVINE GREENS

We commonly use the term "communities" when talking about groups of people. Only rarely do we think of other animals as having the sophistication to form such complex entities. And never plants. But plant communities are common and necessary to the well-being of all us rootless ones.

For instance, trees that prefer the same types of soils, dry or wet environments, locations and climatic conditions such as north- or south-facing hillsides, will tend to grow together. In this part of the continent, where you find maple trees you'll probably also find beeches and probably oaks as well. If they're growing on the south side of a ridge or ravine, there may well be a hemlock forest on the north side.

Scientists studying the interdependence of species have customarily referred to the entire grouping of trees, shrubs, herbs and mosses as a community. Recently, a more comprehensive designation has come into use that includes every living and non-living thing in the environment. This incorporates animals in all their diverse forms and sizes, both alive and dead, as well as plants, soils and climate. The whole bundle of interacting parts is referred to as an ecosystem. In this sense, the organic and inorganic components constitute the structure of the ecosystem, while the interacting forces of productivity, consumption, competition and cooperation are the dynamics of the system.

When you look closely, you'll see that in a forest there are multiple layers of life working together in harmony. This layering from root tip to treetop enables different species to occupy the same space without competing with one another.

There are some who believe that the soil, the dirt, that stuff beneath your feet, is mainly good for holding timber roots in place, mining minerals out of, or sinking building foundations down into. It's inorganic, they say, a kind of neutral matrix on top of which the interesting stuff happens. This is the attitude that leads to the belief that we can just bulldoze the stuff into different forms with impunity, that we can spray deadly toxins on top of it and affect only the insect or plant visible in the sunlight. This attitude is uninformed, shallow and wrong.

In fact, the soil layer is the source of most of the nutrients that make life on the land masses of the planet possible. It nurtures and is home to billions of organisms, large and small, which in total constitute a surprisingly large part of the entire biomass. It also provides shelter for a host of burrowing animals, including groundhogs, cottontail rabbits, moles, muskrats and many more. When it's time to give birth, foxes and wolves go to earth. When it's time to hibernate, bears find a cave. Earthworms and other invertebrates constantly churn the soil, mixing, enriching, and aerating it, and bringing nitrogen down into it for better plant growth.

Atop the soil, and blending into it, is the litter layer, where all the dead leaves come to rot. And it's not just leaves. Except when there's some sort of burial, or the end product reaches water, all life ends up as litter sooner or later. There's always leaf mould, dead plants, fur, feathers and feces being broken down into soil components by micro-organisms. In addition to the plants, there are also various fungi and swarms of tiny litter-dwelling creatures living, dying and reproducing here in the millions.

Next up comes the field layer. Here grow the herbaceous plants, moulds and lichens. In spring you'll see hepatica, trilliums, false Solomon's seal, and all the other spring flowers, rushing to make fertile seed before the leaves emerge up above. In summer, wherever there's enough light and a little boggy ground, glistening jewelweed grows, otherwise known as spotted touch-me-not. Where the woods are denser and limbs and leaves form a thick canopy high above, ferns and mosses run riot. In the open fields beside the woods is the layer that contains most of the plant growth.

The smallest of the permanent mammalian residents, the mice and shrews, and occasional salamanders are often the hardest to see, except when they're dead. The larger animals such as the foxes and raccoons pass through forests, usually on their way somewhere else. Much of the hunting and killing by the larger lifeforms, both birds and animals, takes place in this layer, both in the open fields and beneath the trees. Especially in winter, white-tailed deer may search desperately here for twigs to browse or last season's grass not too deeply buried, or just for a place to find protection from arctic winds.

Few if any birds live on the forest floor anymore since the bobwhites and wild turkeys disappeared, but sometimes ovenbird or partridge are seen. Robins will drop in to feed on the smaller lifeforms that abound here. And, of course, squirrels gather much of their diet here, and warehouse it here as well.

The next layer is the shrub layer. If the tree cover isn't too dense there will be a layer of bushes, shrubs, taller woody plants and small trees. There may be raspberry and nettles growing in any more open spots, waiting to scratch your bare human legs or tear at your trousers. In late June or early July they can also provide a delightful feast. In the meantime they spend their lives growing and reproducing. In a healthy forest, this is also the level where second generation trees get their start. There is ideally a progression in heights and diameters, from seedlings 30 centimetres high to mature trees—in some forests, giants more than two centuries old.

This too is the level at which warblers, woodpeckers, nuthatches and squirrels most actively pursue their business. It is the need to protect this layer and the field layer that makes it necessary to fence off the heavily used stretches of certain park woodlands.

At the top of it all is the forest canopy, where the great trees spread their branches and leaves to take advantage of every ray of sunlight. The lower part provides summer homes for squirrels and occasionally crows. It's here that the birds of prey, the hawks and owls, will alight and watch, watch patiently for the slightest hint of movement below. In these upper branches, the crows roost in winter and make their presence known through the cold air for miles around. In spring and fall, it's also these heights that provide sheltered rest for migrating songbirds. Between and above these upper branches, bats and flycatchers whirl and dart in their search for insect food.

The tree itself is a wondrous lifeform. The visible part is awe-inspiring by itself; a structure perhaps a metre in diameter and approaching 250 years in age, with potentially many more to go. It reaches so high up into the sky and produces so many leaves every year that the mind boggles. But that's only the part you see. Down below is the root system. It's composed of main roots and rootlets of ever-decreasing size, and finally, tiny root hairs. Lay them all end to end and they would stretch for many kilometres. Measure the total surface area and you will find that in most years it exceeds that of all the leaves combined. The purpose of the roots is to absorb water and all the minerals that are dissolved in it, and carry it to the trunk. The trunk in turn transports it up through the layer beneath the bark to the leaves where, with energy supplied freely by the sun, it produces food as various kinds of sugars. These fuel the creation of more leaves, more branches, more trunk, and more roots. Excess is stored in the sapwood just beneath the bark and in the roots, so that there's something there to start from next spring, and to carry the plant through an extra-long winter or drought.

A few years ago there was a severe ice storm in eastern Ontario. Experts said it might take five years to totally assess the damage. The next year there was a drought, and the meaning of the experts' statements became clear. Some trees had lost the capacity to survive severe stress, and they died.

Through the physics of their structure, every day trees gather and lift tonnes of water straight up, perhaps 30 metres or more, and then out through kilometres of branches. The tree needs only a little of the water to keep its leaves from wilting, so most of it is transpired, which in tree terms means about the same as perspired does in human terms. Most of it evaporates from the leaf surfaces, but some also drops back down to the forest floor, which is why you may feel a gentle rain as you walk through the woods on a perfectly cloudless day.

The larger or moving lifeforms are easy to see. To find some others, you'll need to look to death. Though they may look like a wasted resource to a lumberman, dead trees are bounty indeed, life itself to many living things.

When a tree dies, the root system is still in place, and whether or not there are any nutrients left in its structure, it still performs its basic function, transporting water upwards. It's a wick. The result is a long, damp stick of wood, the perfect habitat for a host of organisms. Wood rot and other forms of bacteria break down the structure of the tree into sub-components, resulting in a soft core surrounded by a hard exterior. This can become an ideal nesting site for squirrels and birds. Birds such as woodpeckers and nuthatches search beneath the bark to find the host of organisms that are now growing there.

Many fungi in all their forms live off the remains of trees, whether standing or in the last stages of decay in the litter level. Some specialize, liking only birch or beech for instance. Others are even more picky and may grow on only one old log in a forest.

In time, this stump itself will also fall, or simply disintegrate onto the ground. Even then it will continue to feed a host of other organisms. In addition to becoming a latrine for raccoons, the fallen tree trunk may also become a nurse log to support the growth of other trees or its own offspring. In many of the walks that pass through woodlands, you'll notice big, soft old stumps or rotting logs with all sorts of growth springing up from them, including more trees.

The most important inhabitants of the litter layer are the ones that you're least likely to notice until late summer or the fall. Fungi come in many forms.

Those colourful mushrooms and toadstools you see, especially when the woods become damp and cool in early autumn, are the fruiting bodies of the fungi. Their function is to make and disperse spores, usually from gills on the underside of the caps. Spores are so tiny and light that they will float through the air on the least little zephyr, sometimes alighting kilometres from their source.

It's down below the mouth-watering mushrooms and apparently artificially brilliant slimes that you'll find the hyphea of fungi, that mass of tiny white threads that composes the true fungal body, which carries on the work of decomposition. These fungal threads run in a complex network throughout the soil, and it is they, along with bacteria and other microbes, that account for 80 to 90 percent of all decomposition. In their turn, they become food for the tiny mites, springtails and nematodes.

Before leaving this subject, here are just a few names to contemplate: black-footed marasmius, powder cap, blushing fiber head, alcohol inky, lawn mower's mushroom, golden-gilled gerronema, dung-loving psilocybe, stuntz's blue legs, American Caesar's mushroom, brownish chroogomphus, lead poisoner, viscid violet cort, blue-pored polypore, wolf's-milk slime, moose antlers, tapioca slime, and there are many, many more. It's worth getting a guidebook for the names alone. Just imagine the expression on the faces of the folks back home when you tell them you found witch's butter or scrambled-egg slime in the woods.

There's more to these walks than walking. Stop. Sit. Look. Listen. Imagine and wonder. Begin to understand.

THE DON RIVER
WATERSHED

The Don River flows through the heart of Toronto. It has done so since the town was called York. It has suffered all the indignities that have been inflicted on rivers throughout the Western world. And yet it lives still, some of its valleys still holding places of peace and beauty, its ravines providing homes and food to a host of wildlife. Each of the walks described here is included because it is a good place for humans to spend time, to reflect and enjoy. To ensure that this beauty remains, that these ravines continue not only to survive but actually regain some of their life-enhancing power, it helps to know a little of what's gone before.

A quote from the report of the 1994 Don Watershed Task Force describes the recent situation, and calls for action to reverse the degradation which has occurred. "The Don River, which flows through the heart of Metro Toronto, is one of Canada's most degraded urban rivers. Restoring this watershed to health is a long-term urban renewal project that will mean a new harmony between the area's human communities and natural systems.

"Today, the Don Watershed is 80 percent urbanized and home to 800,000 people. Current population projections suggest that by the year 2021 it will be 91 percent urbanized. Now is the time to change past practices of 'mastering nature' that have characterized agricultural and urban development, and to place the health of the natural system first in planning discussions and daily personal choices."

At the beginning of the third millennium, some are celebrating the rebirth of the Don, and while it is much better than when it was pronounced dead thirty years ago, there's still a long way to go.

The causes were many, and all centred around a combination of an explosion in human population density and a technology that proliferated much faster than its long-term effects could be measured. Both continue.

During the '50s there were two powerful events that shaped the Don into what exists today. One was the aftermath of Hurricane Hazel, and most of the good things that have happened to the Don since that time are attributable to efforts to reduce damage and loss of life the next time there is a similar natural event.

The other occurrence was the construction of the Don Valley Parkway. This roadway is an artery for the city, allowing transportation of all the goods and services vital to life of the city's core. It pollutes the valley both by sight and sound.

Yet there is hope, and there are plans to restore some of the river to its earlier condition. In the long term, it is envisaged that it will be possible to reintroduce wetlands to the river's lower reaches, providing not only wildlife habitat, but also creating a natural filter system for the river's outlet. With determination and constant awareness and effort, it will be possible to regain something, but never to recreate the conditions of two hundred years ago.

The past is gone—we live in the present—but understanding our past can help us shape a better future. Let's take a brief look back in time and space through the eyes of a man who loved the place and devoted much of his life to its preservation, Charles Sauriol. A quote from his *Tales of the Don* takes us back:

> The urge to locate in the Valley was strong. The Forks of the Don in the '20s and '30s was sylvan, serene and naturally beautiful. Huge graceful elms stood along the river banks and on the floodplain, over which cattle roamed. The lofty walls of Tumper's Hill, otherwise known as Greenbank, commanded a view of the four great ravines which met at the Forks of the Don. Some of the Valley slopes were covered with white pine, long since replaced with the deciduous trees of today. Don Mills Road wound its way along the base of Tumper's Hill then, having spanned the Don, pursued its course up and over the rough bricks of de Grassi Hill on to the wooden trestle bridge, whose planks rattled and shook with the impact of each passing vehicle, one perhaps every ten minutes. Three streams met at the Forks: the West Don, the East Don and Taylor Creek. Huddled in the folds of the Valley and tracing the old course of the East Don were several frog ponds.
>
> The sounds, scenes and scents of nature were everywhere, particularly during the spring. Each April dozens of eastern bluebirds dropped from a sky as blue as their wings to perch for a few moments in a row of fence wires. I could catch the scent of the balm of Gilead in the evening air when the sad trilling of the American toads echoed along the deserted Valley, a sound so plaintive that it tugged at one's heartstrings. Sometimes I heard a great horned owl and very often the sweet tremolo of a saw-whet owl.

Much is gone, but fortunately there are still many kilometres of trails offering a host of joys available for living, for a time, with and within nature.

WILD WARDEN WOODS

DISTANCE: 3.5 kilometres

NOTE: Walking is on streets, a paved path and some well-marked trails. There are a couple of high hills. You might want to loop with Don Walk 2 back to Victoria Park, or continue on Don Walk 5 to Eglinton Ravine Park.

GETTING THERE BY PUBLIC TRANSPORT: Take the Bloor/Danforth Subway to the Victoria Park Station. Coming out of the north door of the station, turn right and walk beside the fence. This path will lead down among three highrise buildings. Turn right to the traffic lights at Pharmacy Avenue. Cross at the lights and turn left to a parks department sign reading Warden Woods and Central Don, and their green, white and blue flag. Turn right down to a parking lot.

GETTING THERE BY AUTOMOBILE: Drive along Danforth Avenue and turn north on Pharmacy. As you start down the first hill the Warden Woods sign is on your right just after the traffic lights. Turn right.

SUMMARY: Starts from Victoria Park Subway Station and continues east across Pharmacy Avenue into the park. It goes from the parking lot to a bridge crossing Taylor Creek and following trails beginning beside the creek, and eventually climbing to the western edge of the park, at the top of the old riverbank, then alongside the north side of Taylor Creek to the Warden Subway Station.

THE WALK: In the works yard just before the parking lot, there's a sign reading High Rate Treatment of Combined Sewer Overflows. This is an experiment in solving one of the major problems facing all watersheds in the city—how to clean up storm drain outflow, especially when it's mixed in with overflow from sanitary sewers in flood periods. Wish them well!

Follow the road around and through the parking lot. Here there's a picnic area with barbecue stands.

On the left is Taylor Creek. Down at the waterside it's quite undisturbed, quite "unimproved," and it's very pleasant. The first landmark of note is a storm-sewer cover on a raised concrete base. You'll see a number of these along the paved pathway. In fact you'll see them in ravines in all watersheds. There are often odours emanating from these, usually from sewage, but sometimes from other, unidentifiable sources. On a cool morning, there may often be a cloud of vapour coming off these covers; sniff at your peril. The smell does not come from the creek itself. The creek has many problems, but this isn't one of them.

You'll be walking on a trail paved for cyclists and inline skaters. Be careful—you're at the bottom of a long hill, and cyclists love to coast down at speed. Officially, pedestrians have right of way. In reality, it's hard to see around the corners on some of these curves, and the best advice is to stay on the right side of the pathway and keep an eye open. It is not really dangerous, but caution is advised.

Shortly, both the path and the creek curve sharply to the left. The subway trains up to the right are not as loud as might be expected.

Cross the brown bridge with uprights at each end. This bridge is rotting and may well be replaced in the near future. On the other side, turn right. This wooded stretch is threaded with paths. The following description covers the one that follows closest to the creek.

On the left is the old bank of the original river, preceding the present creek by many thousands of years. There are many places where you can walk down to the water, enjoy the view, or just listen as it burbles over the little rapids. This is a great place for birds all times of the year. There's a plenitude of food, with buds and seeds on the trees, and a host of insects in the trees and among the huge variety of plants growing lushly here. In the winter, it's mainly the seeds, and bugs beneath the bark keeping the birds alive.

There's lots of sumac along here, with berries standing up in their fuzzy dark red clusters. These are reputed to be good for warding off scurvy when boiled up in a tea, because they're full of vitamin C. Chewed in their raw state they have a pleasant, acidic, fruity taste.

Watch for a fork in the trail just after passing over a concrete pipe; it's not always easy to see the trail to the right, but that's the one to follow.

Heading up the main trail again along the creek, especially in the autumn, it's very difficult not to just stop and gawk at the glory of red and gold. You'll come to a partially dead old beech tree with lovely, sensuous grey bark, engraved with lots of carving around the bottom, and rather mammary protrusions further up the trunk. The main path goes on straight ahead, but the one you're following bears to the right.

As the ground continues to rise, you'll come to a high, steep bank falling directly down to the creek below. This makes a great outlook over a crook in the stream; if you're very lucky you might just see a fox or raccoon hunting along the water's edge. If you see a fox, you can be sure the fox sees you. Keep still and don't make a fuss, and the fox will probably just go on about his or her business.

For kids around nine to twelve, this next section is a great climb. For adults thirty-nine and older, it's more of a challenge.

Taylor Creek

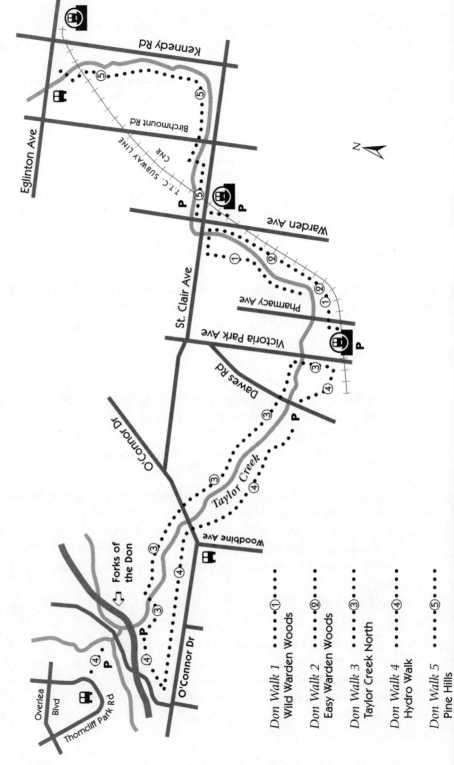

N

Eglinton Ave
Kennedy Rd
Birchmount Rd
CNR
T.T.C. SUBWAY LINE
Warden Ave
Pharmacy Ave
St. Clair Ave
Victoria Park Ave
Dawes Rd
O'Connor Dr
Taylor Creek
Forks of the Don
Woodbine Ave
O'Connor Dr
Thorncliff Park Rd
Overlea Blvd

Don Walk 1 ①
Wild Warden Woods

Don Walk 2 ②
Easy Warden Woods

Don Walk 3 ③
Taylor Creek North

Don Walk 4 ④
Hydro Walk

Don Walk 5 ⑤
Pine Hills

At the top is a chain-link fence. Turn right and follow it. One branch of the path curves off to the left. The more interesting one goes straight ahead over the hill to a good lookout point.

The trail goes up almost to the chain-link fence again and then turns right across an improvised bridge over the trickle at the bottom of the ravine. The "ravine" is no more than a dip in the land here.

Follow the trail to another ravine, then down to the creek again. At the creek, there's a well-defined path going back in the direction you've come from, but following close beside the creek. This trail provides an easy and pleasant side trip, with lots of opportunities to stop and watch, have a snack or just sit.

To continue, turn left and climb a steep incline back up; fortunately there are lots of tree-root steps to provide traction. Follow the trail towards the noise at St. Clair Avenue.

As you walk down St. Clair Avenue, there's a paved path turning down to the right. This is a possible beginning to Don Walk 2. You can follow this to get back to the beginning of the walk. Alternatively, cross Warden Avenue at the lights and turn right to go down to the entrance to the subway station.

GETTING BACK: You're there! You can get just about anywhere on the TTC from here. For drivers, to return to the beginning of the walk take the subway back to Victoria Park, and then follow the directions for Getting There, at the beginning of this walk.

DON WALK 2
EASY WARDEN WOODS

DISTANCE: 3.5 kilometres
NOTE 1: This whole walk is along paved paths, with short side trips as desired.
NOTE 2: This walk may be looped with Don Walk 1 to prolong the pleasure.
GETTING THERE BY PUBLIC TRANSIT: Go to the Warden Woods Subway Station on the Bloor/Danforth line. Take Warden Avenue exit from the station, turn right towards St. Clair and cross to the left at the traffic lights to the sign reading Welcome to Warden Woods, Central Don. Go down the steps.
GETTING THERE BY AUTOMOBILE: Drive to the Warden Woods Shopping Mall at the northeast corner of Warden and St. Clair Avenues. Park as close to the south side as possible, and walk to St. Clair Avenue. Cross Warden to the park entrance on the east side.

SUMMARY: Beginning at the Warden entrance, the walk follows a paved pathway following Taylor Creek to Pharmacy Avenue. There are many opportunities to take side trips to explore flora and fauna or to just sit and enjoy the ambience.

THE WALK: There's been a drive the last few years to replace old wood-pole and earth steps with concrete and an iron rail. Such is the case here. Descend.

From this end of the park, at Warden Woods, the path is always downhill, making it a good family walk or after-dinner stroll. It's also attractive to people on wheels. If walking as a family, keep in mind that some of these turns are tricky to see around, so rather than spreading across the whole path it's advisable to keep everyone to the right so that cyclists can avoid you.

There's a path down to the creek and another paralleling the water's edge as it travels along and makes a long slow curve back towards the paved path.

Numerous paths down to the creek are kept mown during the summer, to allow access to life-saving equipment hung on steel standards. Well, that was the original idea anyway, but there is an ingrained urge in the human species to throw anything moveable into water, so the life rings and long hooked aluminum poles that used to hang on these standards have long since departed downstream. Nevertheless the grass is still cut, providing access to the stream to look, to sit and to enjoy.

Except when the water is high, it's usually possible to find a place to pick your way over stepping stones across to the other side. If you want a secluded spot to enjoy for a while, take one of these opportunities. The risk is a wet foot.

Perhaps a safety note is in order here. Kids love to take off their shoes and wade around in water. Doing that in this water is not recommended, especially if there's a young leg with scratches or a sore on it. Not to put too fine a point on it, this water is polluted.

For those who have just taken the path down from Warden Woods Subway and did not follow Don Walk 1, on your right there's a wide wooden footbridge with brown uprights at either end. This marks the beginning of trails through the woods on the other side of the creek, going back up to St. Clair Avenue and the Warden Woods Station. Check it out sometime.

The path makes one last turn to the right and leads into a parking lot. Walk on through it and up the hill to Pharmacy Avenue.

GETTING BACK: Upon reaching Pharmacy Avenue, turn left to the traffic lights, cross the street and proceed to the first street to the left after Pharmacy. Follow this path to the Victoria Park Subway Station, on the Bloor/Danforth line.

Alternatively, turn left on the western side of Pharmacy, walk under the bridge and then turn right to follow the hydro right-of-way beside the subway line. In time this will also bring you to a subway entrance. Those who left their cars at Warden Woods can take the subway back one stop to that station.

DON WALK 3
TAYLOR CREEK NORTH

DISTANCE: 6 kilometres
NOTE 1: Easy walking for the most part. There are slippery bits in wet conditions, and there are some places where you'll have to climb over trees or crawl under them. There are some hills on side trips if you decide to take them.
GETTING THERE BY PUBLIC TRANSPORT: Take the Bloor/Danforth Subway to Victoria Park Station and exit onto Victoria Park Avenue.
GETTING THERE BY AUTOMOBILE: The parking lot at Victoria Park Station is exclusively for use by subway users. The lots nearest Victoria Park are at Dawes Road, on both sides of the creek. Access to the creek from either location is just a few metres away.
SUMMARY: The walk follows the north side of Taylor Creek where possible, and the paved path on the south side where necessary. It leads to the Forks of the Don and can be looped with Don Walk 4, returning on the other side of the valley.

THE WALK: Coming out of the Victoria Park Subway Station, turn right down to the traffic lights, cross, turn right and continue to a flight of steps (fifty of them) down to the valley floor. There's a brown sign at the top with a symbolic representation of someone walking and another pointing down the valley—it reads Edwards Gardens 10 Kilometres.

Down at the bottom there are a pair of graceful weeping willows. They'll be a common sight on the walk, but none the less attractive for that.

The usual paved path caution for walkers applies here. The path is used by cyclists, inline skaters, joggers and walkers, and the traffic gets pretty heavy sometimes, especially on weekends. If there are children along, try to keep the family on the right-hand side of the path. Or why not walk on the grass?

The small field between the path and that north bank is soggy most times of the year, as evidenced by extensive stands of cattails. Red-winged blackbirds love them in spring and early summer, and raucously defend them against all comers and each other. Beyond the cattails, the flat land is dotted with planted trees.

Just past Dawes Road Bridge there is a footbridge leading to the left into a parking lot. This is not the path we're taking, but there is a restroom here. It's open all year too. This will be the starting point for anyone who has parked nearby.

After crossing beneath Dawes Road Bridge, at the same point where the footbridge leads over the creek, there is a path straight ahead and another up to the parking lot on the right. The one straight ahead soon leads into brambles and fallen trees. Follow the one to the right.

Turn to the left at the top and walk along the edge of the parking lot. At the end of the swimming pool and the black chain-link fence, turn left down the hill to the creek. Follow the trail and take the first fork to the right.

The foundations of the city expose themselves on the other side of the creek. On top there is a thin layer of earth, then a thicker layer of red clay, and finally, clearly stratified layers of grey clay on its way to becoming shale, then real shale all the way down to the water. Occasionally you might also see half a tree's root system exposed as the surrounding soil slowly erodes away.

Before reaching the next footbridge, bear right through the bushes to the open park beyond. There's a sign marked Halsey. This is the beginning of the promenade part of the walk. What began as a narrow trail soon broadens out into a wide path.

The next footbridge carries a pathway up to a residential area on the right. There are a number of flat, mown lawns along this section of the trail, offering the opportunity to sit down for a while, play frisbee, or let the dog chase squirrels.

It pays to look down into the water from time to time; there are actually quite a number of fish in this part of the creek, including suckers up to 30 centimetres or more in length. Patience is required, and a pair of polarised sunglasses help to see beneath the water's surface.

Another footbridge across the creek carries a path to the right, up a set of steps, past a park bench, and on to street level.

Throughout this whole ravine there are a wide variety of birds disporting themselves in the warmer months (200 different kinds have been reported). They are especially evident in the spring and early fall, when all these ravines and valleys become migration flyways. Occasionally an early-morning visitor will be rewarded with the sight of a fox or raccoon, or possibly a weasel.

The next in this series of footbridges is actually part of the trail, and crosses not the creek, but a small stream running down from the right. There are trails up both sides of this stream, well worth an exploratory side trip.

Just after this crossing is a place where erosion has proceeded to the point where the bank is now at the very edge of the trail. There's a row of gabion baskets leading down into the water and forming one side of a quiet pool.

On the other side of the next bridge there's a sign pointing across in this direction; it reads O'Connor Drive & TTC, and below it, Glenwood Crescent. Just beyond, along the paved path and to the right, is another public washroom, open in summer only.

The trail from here on will become a little more challenging, and more interesting. It narrows right down from a broad, mown passage to a narrow footpath. Continue on towards the O'Connor Bridge. The trail forks, the right one going up towards the road and the 70 O'Connor bus running to the Coxwell Station on the Bloor/Danforth Subway line. The left, less-used fork slopes down towards the creek. The trail under the bridge itself can be muddy at times, so detours are allowed, even recommended.

Past the bridge, the trail dives into dense growth again, and winds around and up and down extensively. It then makes a sharp turn directly downhill. When wet, it's slippery, so watch your step. At the bottom there's a trail running along the edge of the creek.

Just before the next footbridge there's a bit of a scramble to get up and over an overgrown bank. The paved path has now crossed from the south to the north side of the creek. This is the first of two footbridges across the creek. The creek's now on the left.

The second bridge crosses not the main creek, but a smaller stream coming down from the north in its own little ravine. Here's another interesting side trip. Just follow the trail up the west side of the stream and then on up the hill. At the top it curves to the right behind backyards, and eventually it curls back around to the trail at an earlier point.

At the next bridge stay on this side for now.

Just before the following, and last bridge, there's a picturesque picnic ground with a firepit and benches, surrounded by tall old trees. There's also a path going up the side of the hill on the right. This and others around here can provide a final chance for some personal exploration.

Do cross this bridge, and turning right, you'll find yourself in a parking lot. For those wishing to return to the beginning by a southern trail, see Don Walk 4. For those wishing to get to the TTC, read on.

Approaching the Don Valley Parkway at four or five o'clock in the afternoon makes you abundantly conscious of what has been left behind. The roar and rumble of heavy trucks, the great diesel moans of busses, the scream of an emergency vehicle. These and more ram their way into your senses, leaving no room for the marvellous mathematics of the veins of a leaf, or the insistent energy of a wren silently seeking seeds.

Cross an old concrete bridge over Taylor Creek for the last time. Here it joins up with the East or Little Don River, and just a bit further downstream past the Don Valley Bridge the combined streams flow into the Don River at a place known since the time of the earliest settlers as the Forks of the Don.

Follow over the railroad track to another parking lot. To reach the TTC, turn left and follow the road parallel to the railway tracks, then turn right up the hill leading to Thorncliff Park Drive.

GETTING BACK: Catch the Thorncliff Park 81 bus running to the Pape Subway Station of the Bloor/Danforth line. After 3:30 P.M., it stops on this side of the street. Before 3:30 P.M., it stops on the other side of the street, going in the other direction. Why? Only the TTC knows! If your car is at the Victoria Park TTC lot, take the subway from Pape east to Victoria Park.

DON WALK 4
HYDRO WALK

DISTANCE: 7 kilometres
NOTE: Some moderate hill-climbing is required, and there are sometimes numerous muddy patches. The trail is usually clear, but autumn leaves or snow may obscure it in places near the beginning.
GETTING THERE BY PUBLIC TRANSIT: Take the Bloor/Danforth Subway to Pape Station. Then take the Thorncliffe Park 81 bus to Thorncliffe Park Road where it turns right. Get off where a sign reads E. T. Seton Park, Central Don. Go past the sign and down a paved road. This road is frequently used, especially weekdays, so keep well left and avoid unpleasant surprises.

At the bottom of the hill the road splits, the right-hand way leading to a parking lot and picnic ground. Turn left, towards a different parking lot.
GETTING THERE BY AUTOMOBILE: Take the Don Valley Parkway and exit to Don Mills Road North. Keep to the right on the curve of the cloverleaf, and take the first exit on the right, marked Taylor/Massey Creek Park. Follow the road under the parkway to a parking lot.

SUMMARY: This walk takes you from the Forks of the Don along the south side of Taylor Creek, mostly beneath the hydro right-of-way, to Victoria Park.

THE WALK: This first section is for public transit users. Car drivers can start from the parking lot. Crossing the bridge to the parking lot, the Don Valley Parkway Bridge and a railway bridge are on the right. All three bridges are spanning the East Don River. Just a little further downstream it joins the West Don and Taylor Creek to form the Don River. Logically enough, this junction has been known for a century and a half as the Forks of the Don.

Signs ahead point to the left to Edwards Gardens, 5 kilometres, and Sunnybrook, 5 kilometres. Cross the railway tracks on the footbridge. Don Valley Parkway is to the left, Don Mills Road to the right, and the Valley of Taylor Creek is ahead.

In the parking lot after the bridge, about halfway down to the right, there's a bronze plaque. It gives a brief history of the Charles Sauriol Conservation Reserve and presents an indecipherable map. There's a path into part of the reserve leading off the other side of the parking lot. It leads eventually to Eglinton Avenue, and is a trail you might want to explore some time. The most interesting walk is through the northern portion of the reserve—see Don Walk 12.

In addition to this nature reserve, Charles Sauriol is remembered for the books he wrote on the early pioneer life on and around the Don River. He describes a river and a way of life almost unrecognizable today. These books are readily available in Toronto's public libraries.

Proceeding south, cross an old concrete bridge to the Elevated Wetlands Project. Turn left here, under the bridge and into the parking lot. Keep to the right—this roadway is used by cars, trucks, motorcycles, cyclists, skateboarders, inline skaters, dogs, foxes, baby carriages and pedestrians.

This is the starting point for those who came by car.

Leave Taylor Creek now, walk to the far end of the parking lot and follow the path leading off to the right. This large meadow is criss-crossed with paths. Walk towards the farthest corner.

After crossing a small stream, start up a hill, paralleling the road. Stick to the right-hand path until you come to a large, rather beat-up looking tree, by far the largest tree around, with a trunk more than half a metre thick. Just past it, turn up the hill to the left.

Now among somewhat older trees you can begin a slow upward climb. There are oak, beech, birch and many maples—a healthy forest. The trail meanders along the side of the old bank, beginning to circle around the valley. There are many mostly dry gullies running down this bank. A line of wooden hydro poles crosses the path. It's hard to see through the leaves in summer, so watch for a trail branching off to the right and leading uphill. Go straight ahead here under the wires, over an iron sewer grating, and across a little streamlet. The path is now beginning to curve to the left, around the edge of the valley.

There are some places along here which in damp weather can be slippery and tricky, with lots of little dips and hollows.

After having circumnavigated the valley and negotiated a deep dip, scramble up to a plateau running under the hydro power pylons. Turn sharply right to follow these lines along a little valley about halfway up the old embankment. There are many muddy little dips in this trail, too many to mention individually. Watch your step.

Many of the spaces along here are now filled with cattails and marsh grass. This whole area is made muddy by little streams seeping out of the bank higher up, where gravity starts dragging them down to the creek. During the day there's little evidence of animal life, but a whiff of something once in a while suggests a hidden skunk, or more likely a fox. This is perfect hunting terrain for foxes. There are a number of side trails along here well worth exploring.

At the O'Connor Drive Bridge if you're tired, bored, or hungry, scramble up to road level and board a 91 Woodbine bus south to the Woodbine Subway Station, or a 70A O'Connor bus south to Coxwell Station, both on the Bloor/Danforth Subway line. Otherwise, turn left and follow down beneath the bridge to the paved pathway, the domain of bikes, trikes and joggers.

Just after the bridge there's a washroom, and on the corner a water fountain. Both are out of commission half the year due to the polar proclivities of our climate. But they do provide welcome relief in their season. Starting at the water fountain, take the long paved pathway angling up the side of the hill. Partway up, there's a short flight of stairs leading to Stan Wadlow Park and Memorial Arena.

Cross the parking lot and follow a footpath leading towards the hydro right-of-way. When the trail splits, take the branch that follows the hydro lines

Just before reaching the apartment buildings at Eastdale Avenue, a mown field and a large transformer station, there's a paved roadway. Follow it up a little hill to the right of the station. Pass True Davison Acres on the left, and continue on to Dawes Road. If you came by car, turn left down to the parking lot.

Cross Dawes Road (careful, it's busy), jog a little to the right, and continue on into a park. There are a couple of routes along here; just stay under the hydro lines. Eventually you'll come to a covered bridge over Victoria Park Avenue, right into the subway station.

GETTING BACK: From Victoria Park Subway, go anywhere on the TTC.

DON WALK 5
PINE HILLS

DISTANCE: 4 kilometres
NOTE: This is an easy walk, on clear paths and trails.
GETTING THERE BY PUBLIC TRANSPORTATION: Take the Bloor/Danforth Subway to Warden Woods Station. Exit at the Warden Avenue door and turn right to the traffic lights at St. Clair Avenue.
GETTING THERE BY AUTOMOBILE: Drive to the corner of Warden and St. Clair Avenues. Go north to the entrance to the parking lot for the Warden Woods Mall. Park as far south in the lot as possible, close to the covered pedestrian overpass to the subway. Walk through the overpass to ground level and go back to St. Clair Avenue and turn left to the traffic lights at Warden Avenue.
SUMMARY: The walk follows along St. Clair Avenue to the right, to the entrance to the St. Clair Ravine. After passing the park entrance, it follows the path along beside Taylor Creek to Birchmount Road. After Birchmount, it proceeds along the Nature Trail in the Pine Hills Cemetery. After leaving the cemetery, it continues along the path beside the creek to Eglinton Ravine Park and Eglinton Avenue.

THE WALK: Cross St. Clair Avenue, turn right and proceed down the hill to the left. Continue under the subway underpass and turn left at the sign marking the entrance to the St. Clair Ravine. The paved path continues along the left side of Taylor Creek until it reaches Birchmount Road. You should cross over the creek to the right, and follow it along on that side.

The creek is very still, slow moving and relatively deep in here. The path is perhaps 2.5 metres wide and surrounded on both sides by grasses and other vegetation. At almost any time of year there are extensive growths of dog strangling vine. In some cases the vine can become dense enough to kill the plants supporting it, though this happens only occasionally. Wild grape can, of course, be even more deadly because of its larger leaves, and it's able to smother and kill good-sized young trees.

Another paved path from St. Clair crosses the stream on a steel footbridge, and continues up to the residential area on the left. From the centre of the footbridge, the view in both directions is picturesque and deserves a few moments' quiet contemplation. Finally the paved path and the trail meet at the corner of St. Clair and Birchmount Avenues.

Cross Birchmount at the traffic lights, angle a little to the left, and enter the Pine Hills Cemetery. Please bear in mind that this is a cemetery, and although you will rarely be within sight of actual burial ceremonies or mourners, it's a place of great emotional significance to many people.

Follow a paved path for a ways, much of it screened off from the rest of the cemetery by trees. As the creek begins to bend north from St. Clair Avenue, the path starts to descend into its valley. The trees close in and there are bushes on both sides.

You'll come to a small concrete bridge, more pleasing to the eye than the usual functional municipal bridge. It brings vehicular traffic across the path as a part of the cemetery road network. Across this road, a little to the left, a wooden structure marks the entrance to the Nature Trail, as this path is known within the cemetery.

Cross the creek on a steel footbridge; the path is again lined and in places overhung with trees. This trail through Pine Hills Cemetery is probably one of the most attractive woodland paths in the city.

When the path splits, take the one to the left and down a set of steps. Next, mount a set of steps and cross a concrete bridge to the left: there's another Nature Trail sign pointing the way. Just beyond this there is a field artillery piece from the Second World War, set here as a monument to all those killed in the conflict.

Cross the road and walk along a bank midway between the upper bank to the left and the creek bank below.

Soon the most-travelled path climbs to the left and continues along the edge of the cemetery proper. Another trail to the right continues along this flat, however it's frequently very wet. Unless you're wearing waterproof boots, you could be squelching for the rest of the day. You can go up and walk along the grassland's verge or continue along the wet way. This whole stretch is filled with tall water-loving plants and grasses. Soon this path too climbs a short incline and meets up with the other one beside a bridge.

Cross the bridge and turn left here, and in a few moments you are out of the park, following a trail along a chain-link fence to the left.

This completes the most scenic part of this walk. It's possible to turn to the right here, walk over to Kennedy Road, cross over and catch the 113 Danforth bus northbound to the Kennedy Station on the Bloor/Danforth Subway line.

For those continuing on, cross the street, then the creek, and go on down the hill to the right into a small park. Cross the next street, keep to the right, and follow the creek.

The creek is becoming small. Many little culverts, each contributing its trickle, have cumulatively built the full creek. Originally, a hundred or more years ago, there was a myriad of little creeks and streams feeding in, but over the years, with each new housing development, more and more have been forced into culverts and hidden away, until all that is left are these ragged pipes sticking out of the bank.

Yet another steel footbridge carries a path between two groups of homes; keep to the right beside the creek.

There's a steep climb to a CNR spur line. Go past the fence on the left, and follow the trail up to the left to where it makes a sharp right turn. Cross a little gully and then climb a bank to the railway right-of-way. Looking carefully in both directions, cross the three sets of track, and go through the fence. Keep to the right, avoiding the path leading off to the residential community on the left. At the top of the hill, take the path leading on to the creek.

At the next fork take the right path, descending to Taylor Creek. It might now be more accurately called Taylor Stream. Cross on the stepping stones provided, and go up into Eglinton Ravine, the small park that marks the end of the walk.

The creek continues north from here, first through an industrial development and then a residential area, almost to Highway 401. Through the industrial area it is strictly controlled in a concrete channel, after that it often disappears underground or trickles through backyards. In any case it does not provide pleasant walking.

There's a huge old gnarled willow tree on the left, and the creek disappears into a great concrete portal. The street ahead is Eglinton Avenue and this is the end of this walk.

GETTING BACK: Walk up to Eglinton Avenue, and just to the left is a bus shelter where you can catch a 34 Eglinton Avenue East bus to the Kennedy Station on the Bloor/Danforth Subway line. To return to a car left at Warden Woods, take the subway back and leave by the exit leading to the Warden Woods Mall.

EAST DON PATH

DISTANCE: 6.75 kilometres

NOTE: This walk along paved pathways is for just about anyone: it makes no excessive physical demands.

GETTING THERE BY PUBLIC TRANSIT: Take the Yonge Street Subway to Sheppard Station and then the 85 Sheppard East bus to Leslie. Cross to the north side, turn left then right at the sign that reads East Don Parkland. Walk down into the parking lot.

GETTING THERE BY AUTOMOBILE: Drive to the corner of Sheppard Avenue and Leslie Street. Go west on Sheppard to the first turnoff at a sign, East Don Parkland. Almost immediately, turn right again into the parking lot.

SUMMARY: The walk travels north along the paved pathway, crossing the footbridges as they occur, with the exception of an old bridge with an iron railing that carries a path leading left up the East Don. It continues to the right on the paved path, and follows it up to where it exits onto Leslie Street.

THE WALK: The good news is that there is a washroom right at the parking lot; the bad news is that it's closed for half the year. Someone with a sense of humour once chalked a message on the wall: Closed for the Season, Freezin' is the Reason. What it lacks in elegance it makes up for in informational content.

Just before the parking lot, turn left onto a paved pathway that you'll follow all the way to Steeles Avenue. Following a paved path is not customary in these walks, but there's no practical alternative to experience the lands on the east side of the river. Just be wary of bikes: they're often very quiet. There are numerous opportunities to wander off on side trails—take some.

The path soon curves to the right over a footbridge, and downriver there's the remains of an abandoned dam; the water now goes around rather than over it.

Across the bridge, turn left. The path makes a sharp curve to the right, and immediately after there's a more interesting, unpaved trail off to the left beside the river.

After that bridge, way up in the middle of the air, behold—a railway bridge. With luck you'll get to hear a train passing over. Don't worry; you won't miss it. Several tons of iron rolling on steel wheels over a steel bridge will never sneak past when you're not paying attention.

The next footbridge will be the last one for a while, so why not take a moment to stand in the middle and enjoy the view in both directions. There's a good chance of seeing, or at least hearing, a blue jay or cardinal, and usually there's a quacking mallard or two somewhere about.

Further along there's an example of how wild animals insert themselves into the middle of an urban environment. From time to time a pair of beavers discover a little trickle of water running through the boggy section to the right, and decide to do some pioneering work. And sometimes an outlet is visible quite close to the path at the south end of the dam. If you're prepared to brave the muddy patches, you can follow the trail leading around part of the pond to the right. On the side opposite the paved path you'll find a considerable stretch of dam. Further along yet is the beaver hutch itself.

Whether or not there are beaver, there are usually a couple of muskrats about. They build their hutches from cattails and grasses, often on muddy flats at the north end of the pond.

Besides the beaver there are usually at least a few mallards swimming around dabbling for greenery on the bottom. Once a great blue heron was seen spearing a goldfish. How such an exotic fish ever got into this muddy pond is a mystery; they're certainly not natives. There are often twenty, thirty or more of these large, healthy aliens to be seen, flashing beneath a flock of begging ducks near the edge of the pond. They do quite well on the food the ducks miss. On the other hand, herons of both the great blue and night varieties are more common visitors. If you want to see patience in practice, watch a hunting heron.

Just past the tennis courts (Alamosa Park), there's a path going up the hill to Alamosa Drive. Continue on down to the left.

In the snow months all this stretch is a great place to look for the tracks of mouse, fox, raccoon, and coyote. Even in the warm months, muddy riverbanks hold impressions of the visitors' feet, telling their stories of hunting, resting, drinking.

Look for a classic Canadian pine tree, looking like something from a Tom Thomson painting. It was because of trees such as this that much of the country north of here was first settled. Loggers went into the bush to cut trees to build the English navy, farmers went in behind to grow food to sell to the loggers, and eventually storekeepers and resort operators went in to serve the tourists who came to see where the big trees had been. White pines can grow up to 30 metres tall and about a metre in diameter.

Round a curve, and heading off to your right is the path up to Finch Avenue and the 39 Finch East bus. It will take you west to the Finch Subway on the Yonge

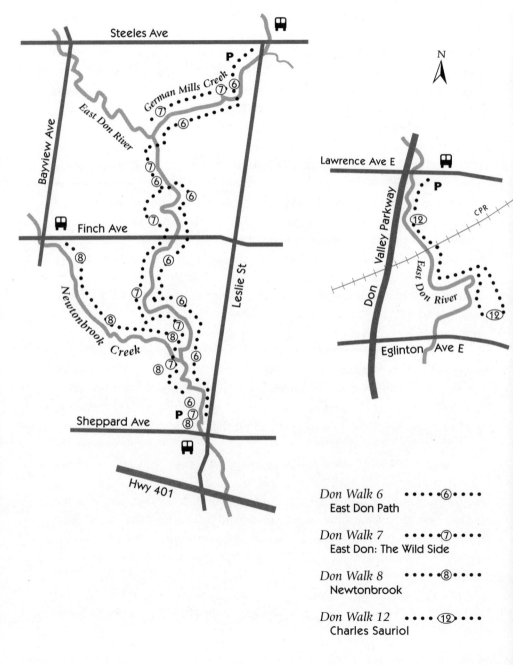

N

Don Walk 6 ••••• ⑥ ••••
East Don Path

Don Walk 7 ••••• ⑦ ••••
East Don: The Wild Side

Don Walk 8 ••••• ⑧ ••••
Newtonbrook

Don Walk 12 •••• ⑫ •••
Charles Sauriol

Street line, if you want to end your walk now. On the other hand, if you're still enjoying the experience, bear off to the left beneath the Finch Avenue Bridge.

At the hydro right-of-way there are three rows of towers running off in both directions. Here there's a refurbished concrete footbridge to let you cross without a drop of river on your shoes. Just before this bridge, there's a smaller one across a little stream, both sides of which are thoroughly boxed in with gabion baskets.

On the other side of the Cummer Avenue Bridge, a paved path goes up to the left, offering another opportunity to catch a bus, this time the 42 Cummer bus, which returns to the Finch Subway Station at the top of the Yonge Street line. Continue on straight ahead.

There's a short stretch of woodland here and a bench for resting just before you turn sharply to the right over a steel footbridge to the east bank of the East Don. Yet another classic view.

After the bridge, turn left at a path coming down from the roadway up above. You're still following the river. On your left is an old, short, footbridge with an iron railing, crossing a stream much reduced from the one you've been following. You have left the East Don River and are now travelling along German Mills Creek. It was named after an early settlement north of here created by a group of German immigrants who built a mill.

Next the trail passes under an elevated footpath crossing the whole width of the valley. Up ahead, another elevated railway bridge signals the end of the walk.

When the valley narrows, cross the bridge over the stream, and follow the path around to the left. Just on the other side of the bridge, there's a path angling back to the left. That's the real beginning of Don Walk 7.

The path slowly and gently curves to the right, between trees and a constantly changing parade of green growth, towards the end of the walk. At the entrance to the trail from Leslie Street there are two huge old weeping willows. You might want to take a moment at the picnic table to sit, eat the last of your snacks, or just rest before turning around to venture out on Don Walk 7, a walk on the wild side.

At Leslie Street turn left and go up to Steeles Avenue.

GETTING BACK: Cross Steeles to the north side and take the 53 Steeles bus west to the Finch Subway Station. For those who left a car down at the beginning, wait for the Leslie bus just south of the corner and take it back down to Sheppard Avenue.

EAST DON: THE WILD SIDE

DISTANCE: 7 kilometres

NOTE: The first section of this walk follows relatively open paths offering easy walking. The second part, however, follows trails sometimes indistinct, occasionally invisible, and frequently difficult. Footing is often muddy and slippery, and waterproof footgear is strongly advised. You may have to jump and clamber in a couple of places.

GETTING THERE BY PUBLIC TRANSIT: Take the Yonge Street Subway line to Finch Station and then take the 53 Steeles Avenue bus to Leslie. Alternatively, take the 81 bus from Eglinton Station travelling up Leslie to Steeles. Go south on Leslie Street past Equestrian Court to the paved path entrance to the right. There's a small picnic spot to the left of the path.

GETTING THERE BY AUTOMOBILE: There's a small parking area right at the entrance on Leslie just south of Steeles. There is also a TTC parking lot at the Finch Subway Station; it may be easier to park and go TTC.

SUMMARY: Starts from the paved path running off Leslie, taking the trail leading to the right just before the first footbridge; it follows a number of trails and tracks, first down the west side of German Mills Creek and then along the East Don River to Sheppard Avenue at Leslie.

THE WALK: As with most of the paved pathways in Toronto parks these days, this one is increasingly well used, in summer especially, so watch out for people on wheels.

In this first section you can begin identifying wildflowers in the warmer months. One of the more spectacular, because of its size, is the teasel. It's a kind of thistle having a spiky domed crown. When in bloom, the top is made up of many tiny lavender flowers, with long spikes in between. From a distance the effect is that of a beautiful silver purple colour. It stands between 1.5 and 2 metres in height, blooms between June and October, and the brown husk will stand all winter. The leaves clasp the stem so tightly that they actually hold little puddles of water on a dewy morning, quickly creating a mini-habitat for insects. This plant, like so many that we take for granted, is an alien. Although the first Europeans brought many undesirable things to North America, certainly we are far richer for many of the flowers that were not here a couple of hundred years ago.

Just before the footbridge, leave the path and follow a trail angling up to the right along the west bank of the German Mills Creek.

Along the creek banks, tree roots bind the soil and clay to form vertical walls. They've resisted chunks of ice and debris tumbled along by high water for many years. These binding forces existed long before we dumped stones in the creek to do the same job. For this reason it is important that trees and bushes be allowed to grow along stream banks.

One downside of walking here in the leafy months is the nettles. They grow to a metre or more in height and have dark green, deeply serrated leaves. Even the slightest casual brush with a finger can still sting hours later. The best cure is avoidance: wear long pants and try to keep bare arms and hands above waist height. Rubbing with crushed jewelweed helps.

As you walk through a damp patch with cattails and milkweed growing profusely, up above is a long footbridge crossing the whole width of the valley, knitting both sides of the human community together.

When the trail forks just before a stream, take either one—they come to the same place. Walk across the stream on stepping stones, and up the other side using root steps.

Anyone looking for a diversion can explore beside the stream, up the ravine on either side as far as Bestview Park, where there are a number of other scenic trails to be explored.

To continue, stay fairly close to the river. A row of posts marks the entrance to a wider gravel-covered trail. Follow it to the left, passing a row of posts, while the trail continues to widen. The vegetation has been trimmed back to make the path about 1.5 metres wide.

At the confluence of the German Mills Creek and East Don River flowing in from the right, cross to the left on the old footbridge, to the other side of German Mills Creek, and continue for a while down the paved path beside the East Don to the high overpass at Cummer Avenue.

Just before reaching the bridge, go up the path to the right and, carefully looking in both directions, cross Cummer. Incidentally, walking up the north side of Cummer would bring you to a bus stop if you wished to terminate your walk here.

On the south side of Cummer, a little to the right, is a path leading down to the flatlands on the west side of the East Don. There's a well-defined gravelled path here. Once again, beware of bikes using this path and keep to the right.

At the hydro right-of-way, turn left and follow the path down towards a concrete footbridge across the Don. This is commitment time. The walk will continue along the west side of the East Don, partway up the hill beneath the hydro towers, then along dim trails through heavy undergrowth, across boggy bits, through a field of leg-grabbing vines and impeding hummocks, and into and through a heavily wooded section pierced by a multitude of little streams with steep high banks. In early summer there are hordes of mosquitoes. It will not be boring. Some would say it's fun and challenging. On the other hand, if you cross the bridge, you could stroll along the paved path down to Steeles Avenue, where there's a washroom and buses, and never even raise a sweat.

If you're still reading, it's assumed that you intend to continue the walk as described. Turn right onto the trail that continues along both the river and the right-of-way, to the base of a hill, where it forks. Continue straight ahead up the hill along the line where the right-of-way has been cut back. Keep climbing until you almost reach the base of the first tower. Look very carefully to the left between the trunks of the sumacs until you see what might be a trail going down into them; follow it.

This is one of the parts of the walk where the trail can become faint to invisible. But there is a trail here. The overall strategy is to get to the old riverbank on the right, get up it, and then follow close to or at the top of it along to Finch Avenue. If the trail seems to evaporate, just continue south and work your way up the bank.

As the trail rises, it makes an abrupt switchback near the top. It twists, twirls, and twines up towards someone's back door, then swings immediately left again. Just before the trail begins to go downhill towards the sidewalk at Finch Avenue, there's a grove of young pines blocking the trail. Push through them.

Carefully, very carefully, cross the road and go down the bank on the south side, near the end of the bridge, towards the river, to pick up the trail again.

In time you'll come to the first in a series of streams, most being a little too wide to jump easily. With vertical sides and only water and soft mud at the bottom, they present a problem. When the ostrich plume ferns grow thickly, it's quite possible to stumble into one by accident. Cutting up to the right to where the streams are more narrow gives you opportunities to cross. Keep to the trail as much as possible. There is a trail here.

As you come to the end of this runnel-riddled stretch, the river curves sharply to the left, presenting what at first appears to be a 9-metre vertical bank. Don't panic; there is a way. But the next stretch tends to be boggy, so walk carefully.

High on the bluff, looming above, is a large building, light grey and of impressive size. In summer it's mostly hidden by vegetation. Below it the bank falls down to the river, not, as it first appears, vertically, but sharply sloping. As you get closer it's revealed as being passable.

Don't get too far up the bank. If you keep within 3 or 4 metres of the water you'll find a trail along here.

Shortly after you reach more level footing, there's a large field with two big pine trees in the middle of it. One appears to have had its top lopped off at some time. Once again the trail becomes obscure. The field is difficult walking, filled as it is with runnels, hummocks and small gullies. In summer there's also grape vine and dog strangling vine in profusion, making walking difficult and tiring. The grasses grow chest high, and in June and July especially, this field is mosquito ridden. Just take it slow and easy. It's best to keep close to the river on the left where there's usually a trail of sorts; any sort of path will make walking easier.

Around another riverbend, the land to the right looks almost like a park. As you progress, the right-hand bank begins closing in once again. As it approaches the river even more closely, it's scramble time. Partway up, there's a large culvert pouring water down the slope, and the smell of sewage is quite strong at times. It's surrounded by gabion baskets and, once you have made your way up to the first of these, over a steep and (seasonally) slippery slope, it's easy to climb around and over.

Just past that obstacle, there's a broad and gravelled path a metre to the right of the one you've been following, with a short connecting path. Make the switch. The gravel soon stops, just before a stream that's easily forded on stepping stones.

Soon there's another stream to cross, again relatively easily. Now the bank once again comes right down to the river, and there's a really steep little climb to where the trail continues through a grove of sumac at a higher level. Erosion is active here, and keeps chewing the bank away ever closer to the trail. Pulling yourself up by any means at hand is not only permitted, it's advised. Continue through here for a bit, and then down towards a footbridge carrying a paved path over the river from the left. Keep to this path for the remainder of the walk.

Follow along beneath an elevated railway bridge. Cross another footbridge, this time to the left, and follow the path to one last footbridge to the right. Just beyond there's a parking lot. There are some picnic benches here, and you may want to pause for a moment to knock some of the mud off your boots, have a snack and a drink, or use the washroom if the season permits.

Congratulations! If you've kept with it this far, you're a survivor. From the parking lot, go right up a hill, turn left, then left again along Sheppard Avenue to the traffic lights on the corner at Leslie.

GETTING BACK: Take the 85 Sheppard East bus west to the Sheppard Station on the Yonge Street line. If the car's at Finch, take the northbound train to Finch Station. If the car is at Leslie south of Sheppard, take the Leslie bus north.

NEWTONBROOK

DISTANCE: 4 kilometres

NOTE: This trail is clear in all seasons and, except for a short muddy hill stretch near the beginning and a couple of stream crossings on stepping stones, it's easy walking.

GETTING THERE BY PUBLIC TRANSIT: Take the Yonge Street Subway to Sheppard Station and then the 85 Sheppard East bus to Leslie. Cross to the left to the north side, then turn left again until you reach the first right turn with a sign that reads East Don Parkland. Turn here and almost immediately turn right yet again and head on into the parking lot.

GETTING THERE BY AUTOMOBILE: Drive to the corner of Sheppard Avenue and Leslie Street. Go west on Sheppard to the first turnoff (marked East Don Parkland), and almost immediately turn right again into the parking lot.

SUMMARY: The walk follows the paved path to where a trail branches to the left just before the third footbridge. Staying left, it continues north along this well-marked trail beside the creek until it reaches Finch Avenue at Bayview.

THE WALK: There is a washroom just to the right, open in the warm months of the year. The trail leads to the left just before the parking lot.

Turn to the left after crossing the footbridge, and almost immediately pass beneath a GO system railway bridge. Just before the next footbridge, take the trail up to the left through a stand of staghorn sumac and some maples. Whenever it's wet and slippery, grab something and hold on.

Just beyond, there's a stream flowing into the Don. Passing the corner of a chain-link fence, and hopping over a couple of trees, you'll come to a second stream with another easy ford.

There is a path paralleling this one. Don't take it. Refer to Don Walk 7. Continuing on the path, you've left the Don behind and are now following the Newtonbrook Creek.

Judging by the depth of the path along here, it's been in use for many years. Trees on both banks lie where they have fallen, criss-crossing one another, and helping to keep these older, higher banks in place.

Rounding a curve, the flats on this side broaden, and there's a steep hill ahead leading up to a street. The creek crosses beneath the road through two large culverts. Climb the hill, cross the street and descend on a continuation of the paved path down the other side.

There are very few willows along the water on this walk, probably because they like low-lying damp ground, close to water. The old banks along here have been too close to the river, and the actual riverbanks themselves are too high to make willows happy.

Up ahead is the back side of a housing development, and the right bank, also topped by homes, is closing in, signalling the end to this walk. The path narrows and becomes steeper closer to the road. There's nothing like the roar of a passing dump truck to bring you back to reality.

You come out onto Finch Avenue, with Bayview Avenue just to the left.

GETTING BACK: Go to the corner of Finch and Bayview, cross to the right to the north side, and take a westbound 39 Finch East bus to the Finch Subway Station. If the car is back at the beginning of the walk, take the subway south to Sheppard and the 85 Sheppard East bus to Leslie. Cross to the left, the north side, and go back to the parking lot entrance.

There is another alternative for drivers. You could just walk back the way you've come.

DON WALK 9
EARL BALES

DISTANCE: 5.5 kilometres
NOTE: Walking is in all types of terrain, from paved path to stones along a creek bed—usually mostly dry—with some moderate hills. The last few metres are the most difficult, and some brush-bashing is required.
GETTING THERE BY PUBLIC TRANSIT: Take the subway to Wilson Station and the 160 Bathurst North bus along Bathurst to the entrance to Earl Bales Park at the sign, Welcome to Earl Bales Park, West Don.
GETTING THERE BY AUTOMOBILE: Drive along Bathurst to the Earl Bales Park entrance, north of Wilson Avenue. Enter the park at the sign and drive to the parking lot on the right.
SUMMARY: This walk follows a valley east to and around the Toronto Golf Club to the West Don, then heads north to a parking lot at Sheppard Avenue. It then follows Don River Boulevard and various paths and trails north to Bathurst Street. Crossing Bathurst, it follows the roadway down to the river, then follows trails along the east side of the river to Finch Avenue.

THE WALK: It's more pleasant and safer to walk along a winding, paved path just to the right of the road coming in from the entrance.

At the place where the paved path enters the parking lot, stop. To the right (south) is a lawn sloping down to a path, which in turn leads through bushes down into a little ravine. This is not a well-used trail, and it soon meets another trail running at right angles. Turn left and follow it through the trees, halfway down the side of this little ravine. The small stream at the bottom makes a sharp left ahead. Most times this little flow of water is only a trickle, but evidence scattered here and there indicates days of glory past. Knowing how easily and quickly run-off can create a torrent, it's possible to imagine a healthy creek dashing down between these banks after a sudden thaw or heavy rain.

There is no continuous trail down through here, although sometimes there is easy walking along flat sections partway up the banks. Often it's easier to step from stone to stone along the stream bed.

Further along, a gaping hole, barred to branches and large animals, conducts whatever water comes its way into the depths of this woodland for a time. There's no particular reason apparent. Partway up the left bank there is a roadway, unfinished, deeply rutted and boggy, but often drier than the path down below. That's where to continue. The soil here seems to be composed mainly of rotted wood chips and compost—very black and rich looking.

When the stream reemerges, it marries another from the right, and together they pass through a culvert beneath a roughly paved road descending also from the right. The stream turns left, the road follows, and so does the trail.

Ravines such as this may become the hunting ground for sharp-shinned hawks. These birds are most adept at chasing their prey down from the flat, open, urban spaces above, into the trees here below, where they can use their superior manoeuvrability to advantage. They may hunt anything from sparrow up to pigeon size, and when they're finished there will be nothing left except a few feathers. The flying pattern of the sharp-shinned hawk when hunting is flap, flap, flap, flap, glide, rather than the long, circling glide of the more common red-tailed hawk.

At the chain-link fence the path curves to the left along the road, the bank to the left draws away and the land begins to open up. Just beyond a closed vehicle gate, there's a smaller, open gate for people.

Turn through the gate, and leave the road that continues on ahead across a broad field. Turn right along a wide and often-wet path leading east again. The stream still parallels the course, well off to the right, behind a fence.

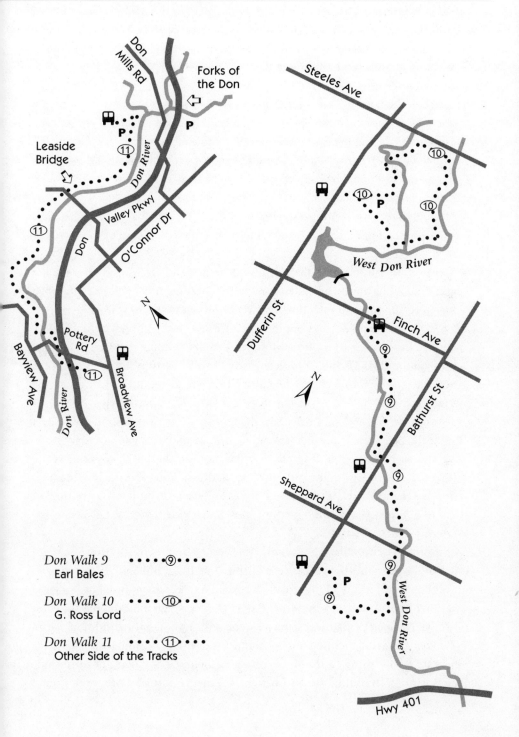

Forks of
the Don

Don Mills Rd

Don

Leaside
Bridge

P

⑪

Don River

Valley Pkwy

O'Connor Dr

Don

⑪

N

Bayview Ave

Pottery
Rd

Don River

⑪

Broadview Ave

Steeles Ave

⑩

⑩

P

⑩

West Don River

Dufferin St

Finch Ave

⑨

N

⑨

Bathurst St

⑨

Sheppard Ave

⑨

P

⑨

⑨

West Don River

Hwy 401

Don Walk 9 • • • ⑨ • • • •
Earl Bales

Don Walk 10 • • • • ⑩ • • • •
G. Ross Lord

Don Walk 11 • • • • ⑪ • • •
Other Side of the Tracks

At the Don Valley Golf Course, turn left at the fence and follow a path which hugs it closely and is separated from the open field to the left by a 2-metre-high berm. The berm makes a great site for groundhog burrows. If a burrow is currently in use, there will probably be some fresh earth beneath the opening; groundhogs are always cleaning and expanding their burrow network, except in winter when they hibernate.

When the fence makes a jog, angle to the left for a bit until you come to a cement footbridge over a concrete-lined stream. The concrete sides run down at a 45-degree angle to a flat bottom. From the middle of the bridge, look to the left along the dead-straight channel. In leafless months you can see that the water is pouring out of a portal halfway up the old ravine bank. This stream is the antithesis of everything natural.

The paved path continues on across a field. Take the other path that runs down from Earl Bales Park at a right angle, paralleling the fence of the Don Valley Golf Course.

The wide path makes a sharp left turn; continue straight ahead on a smaller path, descending a little hill. Take the left fork, heading roughly north through a long green summer's tunnel. It will slowly bring you to the West Don River.

Too soon the trail comes out into the field. The two paths left behind before converge here. The path continues towards a utility building that turns out to be at the bottom of a ski hill, complete with chair lift. Keep to the right along the river. The path begins to climb and curve to the left, to about 6 metres above the water. In the fall, the berry-laden trees across the river attract flocks of cedar waxwings, robins and cardinals. You might want to try a little trail going over beside the river for a while, before coming back to the main path.

At a split in the pathway, the left trail goes up beside Sheppard Avenue along the side of Earl Bales Park, towards Bathurst. You can take the 36 Sheppard Avenue bus back to the Yonge Street Subway, or you could continue on over to Bathurst Street and take the 160 Bathurst North bus back south to the Wilson Subway.

Continue through the parking lot beside and beneath the Sheppard Avenue Bridge, and then bear left to the Don River Boulevard Bridge. Don River Boulevard is not a long street, and you'll quickly reach little Burnett Park, and then the entrance to more parkland. There's a sign announcing the West Don Parklands. The pathway is paved here, and leads to a washroom which is, yes, you guessed it, closed in the winter months. Partway along this path there's a trail leading to the right through a field. Go straight ahead towards the washroom building, then turn right, following part of a big loop around it. Take the first part of the loop, but then take a trail straight ahead, to another trail coming from the east. Turn back west on that one for about 10 metres, and then take a fainter trail off to the right. You should now be heading north, towards a woodland.

Up ahead, a gully cuts through the hogsback, forcing you down to the right. Immediately to the north the path continues back up along the ridge. In a couple of places you'll have to duck or climb over broken limbs.

When the hogsback ends, jog to the left down to the paved pathway. Follow the roadway up the hill to Bathurst, and a little to the right are traffic lights where you can cross.

Straight ahead is the Canadian Jewish Centre complex. Continue by following the road down, keeping well over to the left to avoid traffic. It curves down, continuing all the way behind the buildings. Go straight ahead over the guardrail when the road curves right. That's the last pavement you'll tread until Finch.

A footbridge across the river carries a path that follows the hydro corridor. Ignore it and continue on, angling left towards a structure built into the river. The mowed grass stops, but there's still a trail to follow. This structure is a kind of spillway, with four rows of concrete blocks to deflect the river's powers. The river drops about 6 metres here.

Keep close to the river, beneath a row of hydro pylons. The trail begins to climb up, the trees coming quite close. At the next fork take the right trail, and go down a bank where logs have been inset to form steps.

Take the next right fork. The fork after that is to the left, down a few steps to another trail travelling right along the river. Next, fork left beside the river and along a three-plank-wide duckwalk leading to a broad path cut through the herbs and grasses.

A trail descends from the right to a steel footbridge. There's a sign on the bridge that reads "Welcome to our school. Please start your visit at the office. These premises are monitored by an electronic security system." On weekends, there's a gate across the bridge as well. Bypass both the bridge and the school and continue along the east bank.

Just past the fence, turn sharply to the right up the hill, temporarily leaving the river behind. At the top there's another trail at right angles. Turn left along it.

When you get closer to the river again, you'll find it's way down at the bottom of a steep bank.

The path turns left again. Continue on halfway up the old bank. On the right there is an inscribed beech tree. It's a triple beech in fact, beginning with one base trunk and then splitting into three about 1.5 metres up. Continue along up the hill, and just before reaching a cut in the bank and the buildings, there's a huge old beech tree with swings hanging from it, and the floor of a treehouse in its branches. Cut down to the left around it, through more of the sumac and berry bushes, until you come to a semi-ruined basketball court. Its one intact hoop is still used on occasion. On the far side, at the left corner, there's an old wire fence, and the trail leads down to the river.

In front there's a rapids, and to the right there is a little waterfall. The bank across the river is densely wooded, and there are concrete ruins stretching out of sight to the right. This is a great resting spot. You're getting close to the end of the walk, so this would be a good time to finish off any nibbles that are left, and drink the last of the water.

Following along the river to the right there's only the ghost of a trail, but it is passable. The trail is narrow and up-and-down. This is definitely a one-person path, and you may have to push branches aside in order to pass. Obviously it's not heavily used. At the bridge at Finch Avenue the path moves inland for a little, then down to the left and almost into the river.

You need to go under the bridge, so there's a choice. You can go up to just below where a pipe exits the bank and cross the stream dribbling out of it, or step across stones and patches of grass separating the river from a little backwater. The objective is to get to the bridge.

After the bridge, there's a solid row of townhouses ahead. Bear to the right, leave the path, and keep curving around up the hill until you reach the sidewalk and Finch Avenue.

GETTING BACK: Cross Finch to the south side and take the 36 Finch West bus east. If the car's at Earl Bales, transfer to the 160 Bathurst North bus back south to the park entrance at the next traffic light. If you just want to get back to a subway, stay on the bus, you'll be at the Finch Station of the Yonge Street Subway in just a few minutes.

G. ROSS LORD

DISTANCE: 7 kilometres

NOTE: This walk may have a couple of muddy spots in spring or fall. It follows trails and paved pathways, with only a couple of short, steep climbs.

GETTING THERE BY PUBLIC TRANSPORT:

Monday to Saturday: Take the subway to Downsview Station and then catch the 105 Wilson Heights bus north, up Dufferin Avenue until you come to the traffic lights at Supertest Road. Get off and enter G. Ross Lord Park, West Don. Walk down the left side of this road, past the works department yard, and around to the right to the parking lot.

Sundays and holidays: Go to the Finch Station on the Yonge Subway line and get the 36 Finch West bus to Dufferin. Begin walking up Dufferin to the park entrance, then turn right and walk along the left side of the road to the first parking lot on your left.

GETTING THERE BY AUTOMOBILE: Drive to Finch and Dufferin and then north to the entrance to G. Ross Lord Park at Supertest Road. Follow the road in to the first parking lot on the left.

SUMMARY: The walk follows a series of trails along a part of the reservoir, then up past the horse barns, and east. A path goes up beside Westminster Creek to Steeles, west on Steeles to a path down the West Don, past two bridges, and follows trails eventually leading back to the parking lot.

THE WALK: A cautionary note—you'll be following paved paths off and on during this walk, so please remember that they are heavily used by cyclists and inline skaters during the warmer months; for safety's sake, keep to the right.

From the parking lot, proceed along the road a few metres to a wide trail leading off to the right, marked by a blue arrow on a white square. Follow it down past a ravine through young growth. The next, deeper ravine is the product of a stream you crossed on the way in. Turn left along this one, across yet another small dip, and follow around to the right.

The trail forks and goes right along a less well-trimmed path to a paved trail over a footbridge. It keeps more or less beside the small stream to another up-and-down. Now the footbridge is over to the right, and directly to the left make a short, steep climb to another path on the top of the bank.

The reservoir is up ahead, and further on there are marsh and cattails down to the right about 6 metres.

At the next fork, although there's an arrow pointing left, stick to the right for now. The path begins to angle down towards a pond, a great place to see water-birds in the warmer months. As you curve to the left around this pond you'll come to a stretch where Canada geese spend a lot of time, as evidenced by grass grazed down to the roots, and bushels of goose droppings. This mixture makes for very sticky, slippery walking if the ground is at all wet. A detour may be in order.

Turn up the hill to the left to a wide trail. There are two signs, one reading No Swimming, No Boating, the other, Please Don't Feed Canada Geese. And as you look around at the devastation they have caused, the sign is self-explanatory. Please don't feed them!

A bit beyond this, there's a trail down to the right, following the top of the bank above the pond. When the path forks in various places, continue straight on as far as you can, then switch to the left to another trail. This one carries the imprints of horses' hooves, and there are buildings to the left, which prove to be stables.

Beside the horse trail the sign reads Caution: Do Not Feed or Touch Horses. Although they are not wild animals, horses have been known to bite.

At the triple fork, take the one straight ahead, and then, almost immediately, turn right down the hill through a deep pass into the valley. At the bottom there is a pond on the left, and the end of another pond to the right. Follow the broad trail to the left.

The trail curves to the right through a field and meets another path coming down the hill from the left, then yet another, and finally a paved path. Follow the path over a footbridge. It curves to the left, and there is a branch off to the left over another, smaller footbridge. Continue straight ahead to an unpaved path leading to the right.

There's a small brook to the left. Keep curving in that direction, and continue on past a bridge carrying a path going up to the other side.

One last grand sweep to the left, and a short flick to the right, and you've reached a street. On the other side there is a sign, Festival Park, marking a green passageway between townhouses. There are another couple of these before Steeles Avenue. It's easily recognised by the heavy volume of traffic, and the fact that you can't go any further north.

This walk continues to the left and back down the West Don, but if you wish, you can catch an eastbound 60 Steeles West bus at the bus stop just to the right, back to the Finch Subway stop on the Yonge line.

Turning left then, there's about a five-minute walk down Steeles, to the entrance to a paved pathway along the West Don. The one good thing about this stretch is that the roar of traffic lets you appreciate the relative silence of the ravines all the more. Cross at the traffic light (Hidden Trail), and continue on down towards the valley. Cross the bridge over the West Don, and turn left down the paved pathway into the park.

The valley is narrow at this point; buildings are visible on both sides. It's only minutes before the traffic noise fades. Take the trail leading off to the left towards the river. It curves gently, following the river until it meets the paved path again at a bridge.

A sharp left turn takes you over the bridge into a large field formed by the bowing of the river. Just to the left is a slightly unusual tree, a Norway spruce. Although its needles and general form are that of a spruce, the cones are long, more like those of pine trees. It must have been planted here, because these trees do not occur naturally in this habitat. In their original environment they are valued for the tanning powers of their bark and the spruce beer made from their twigs.

Just beyond a little hump-backed bridge, there's a trail with one of those blue arrow marks, going off to the right. It will take you over to the bottom of the high old riverbank. Follow it along as it curves back, eventually meeting the paved path.

Just before reaching that path, take another trail cutting sharply back to the right again, over towards the old bank, and then up it. The trail leads straight ahead briefly, then left, following the edge of a field. The buildings to the right are interesting, with large round domes and other unusual shapes. They are part of the Canadian Centre for Aerospace Studies.

The trail follows the edge of the field as it curves around to the right, until it reaches what appear to be three large white metal boxes, surrounded by a chainlink fence. Here it changes direction to the left. Walk through an extended grove of small trees and bushes, keeping to the right past a fork.

There's a chain-link fence with an open gate in it, and on the other side there's a trail down to the left. Keep straight ahead. The bank edge drops off sharply, way down to the tableland below.

When you reach the overlook with a bench, down to your left lie the river and the paved path, in front there's another paved path, and to the right are open, mowed lawns and sports fields. Go down the little hill, cross the paved path and, angling a bit to the right, continue up the hill on the other side, following the edge of the grass.

At the corner of the field there's a horse trail in from the right, doing a roundabout here. Follow that back until it eventually swings off to the left between trees, to the paddock you passed earlier. Take the gravel-topped road down towards the large pond.

Instead of staying beside the water, this time take the path that angles off to the right. There are a number of paths through here; they all eventually come to the same place.

The parking lot is up to the right. Join a path coming from the left, and then fork off right again and climb a little hill. Cross another trail into a grove of young trees where there's abundant evidence of horses; don't step in it. At the next cross trail, turn right and come up almost to a road before you turn left. Cross the paved path and continue along this trail, with its groove down the middle, probably created by horses.

Take the next left fork, and follow the trail around by a stream. It curves slowly to the right, to the road and parking lot where you started.

Drivers will here choose to go right; public transit users can turn left and follow the left side of the road around and out to Dufferin.

GETTING BACK:
Weekdays and Saturdays: Cross Dufferin at the traffic lights and go to the bus shelter to the right. Catch the 105 Wilson Heights bus to the Downsview Subway. Sundays and holidays: Turn left and walk down to Finch Avenue and catch the eastbound 36 Finch West bus to the Finch Station on the Yonge Street Subway.

DON WALK 11
OTHER SIDE OF THE TRACKS

DISTANCE: 5.5 kilometres
NOTE: Some hill climbing required—muddy patches in spring and fall. This and adjacent trails are used frequently by mountain bike riders. Stay alert.
GETTING THERE BY PUBLIC TRANSIT: Take the Bloor/Danforth Subway to Pape Station and then get on the Thorncliffe Park 81 bus and take it to Thorncliffe Park Road, where it turns right. Get off the bus at the sign E. T. Seton Park, Central Don. This is the entrance to E. T. Seton Park, Taylor/Massey Creek Park, Wilket Creek Park and the Don River below the Forks.

Go down the road. It's frequently used, especially during the week, so keep well to the left. Rounding a curve to the right there's a great view of the valleys below. Proceed down the hill.

At the bottom the road splits, the right-hand way leading to a parking lot and picnic ground. Go left towards another parking lot. Stop before the bridge.

GETTING THERE BY AUTOMOBILE: Take the Don Valley Parkway and exit to Don Mills Road North. Keep to the right on the curve of the cloverleaf and take the first exit on the right. Continue to an old concrete bridge leading to the left. Cross it and park in the parking lot. Cross the footbridge over the rail line at the end of the parking lot and make a sharp left down the ramp, following the path to where it intersects a road, then turn sharply left to the other side of the bridge.

SUMMARY: The walk follows a variety of trails down the west side of the Don River to where it is crossed by a footbridge, then up towards Bayview and down to Pottery Road.

THE WALK: Starting from the parking lot at the beginning of the bridge, immediately to the right there is a path leading down towards the chain-link fence that marks the edge of the railroad right-of-way. Follow the clear path to the other side of the tracks.

Down to the left is a weir a metre high, challenging to any salmon with spawning in mind. Further on the trail becomes over half a metre deep before turning back down towards the river. At a fork in the trail, stay left and keep beside the river.

Continuing south from the Millwood Road Bridge, cross a large culvert carrying a small stream to the Don. Next is an old wire fence on the left.

To the right is the last remaining sewage treatment facility that empties into the Don. The North Toronto Pollution Control Plant (those green-roofed buildings on your right) is due for an extensive facelift beginning in the year 2000.

The fence makes a right-angled turn to the left. Ignore the path going down to the river on the left and continue on the more well-travelled one. The river once again comes closer, and there's a pipe railing directly above the outlet from the pollution control plant. In colder months the relatively warmer water here attracts a good-sized flock of mallards, who actually swim up into the outlet. Approaching the railing very quietly can result in an explosion of ducks.

Suddenly, on the right, there's a largish pond. It has steep banks all around, and the water level is considerably higher than the river. A 30-centimetre-diameter steel pipe coming up out of the pond suggests that it is connected to the pollution control plant. At times it's home to a million polywogs.

The river now makes a sharp turn to the right, and ahead is a bridge carrying the rail line you have walked beside since the beginning. There is a clear path beneath the bridge, with adequate headroom. There are a couple of paths to the right, but stick to the river path for now. Just before reaching a footbridge, the trail leads up a small bank where it meets a larger path, also following the river. Turn left on this and continue on past the footbridge. To the right there is a long gentle slope, in early summer full of garlic mustard, a green that adds a piquant wild touch to summer salads.

The trail continues past the bridge, then up the hill for a while until you get close to the top. Turn and follow a trail coming down from the right. Take it down into a grove of small trees and then up towards the top. This trail is quite narrow and is intensively used by mountain bikers. They're usually polite and careful, but it's often hard for riders and walkers to see each other until it's almost too late to avoid collision. It's best to give way to the bikes, because it's hard for them to give way to walkers.

Near the end an almost vertical bank takes a bit of negotiating; finding trees or stout bushes to hold on to is a good idea.

When the trail forks, take the one to the left, down a long, gentle slope towards Pottery Road. Eventually you'll reach the flat. Turn left over the tracks, and cross the bridge at Pottery Road.

GETTING BACK: Begin by crossing Pottery Road. Cross over at the paved Don Trail, which runs from Edwards Gardens further north, and continues right on down to Lake Ontario at Cherry Beach. This trail is heavily used by cyclists and inline skaters. Begin to climb the hill up to Broadview Avenue, and you'll soon pass the turn-off to Todmorden Mills Museum—well worth an afternoon's visit with or without children. In addition to the historic buildings, there are some interesting trails through here as well. This was the southernmost of almost forty mills of various kinds that existed in the Don Watershed as far back as the 1850s. It seems that every creek and stream had at least one mill of some kind built on it, employing the free energy source.

Continuing on up the hill, about halfway to the top, look to the right and enjoy the panoramic view of this broad river valley. It has become a communications corridor for the city and its millions of inhabitants. On a clear day you can see the CN Tower down to the left. Nostalgia buffs can also get some feeling for what was lost when this once-green valley was turned into its present form. It's obvious though, that while there's vast room for improvement, there's no going back all the way.

Continue to the top of the hill at Broadview and turn right to the bus shelter. Any bus stopping here will take you to the east-west subway. For those who left their cars at the beginning of the walk, take the subway to the Pape Station, and follow the public transit directions at the beginning of this description.

CHARLES SAURIOL CONSERVATION RESERVE

DISTANCE: 6 kilometres

NOTE: This walk is entirely on trails through mostly wooded and some open areas. There are no cyclists or inline skaters. There are some steep hills and places where the trail may lead along steep banks, so reasonable care is advised.

GETTING THERE BY PUBLIC TRANSPORT: The entrance is off Lawrence Avenue just east of the Don Valley Parkway. From the Eglinton Subway Station on the Yonge Street line take one of the 54 buses eastbound. The first stop after crossing the Don Valley Parkway is Underhill; get off here and walk back down to the entrance. At the sign for Metro Parks and Culture, Charles Sauriol Conservation Reserve, walk in, and down the road to the parking lot.

GETTING THERE BY AUTOMOBILE: Because the entrance is off the south side of a busy street, it's best to come west from Don Mills Road or up from the Don Valley Parkway. The entrance is just east of the parkway, to the right. Drive down the hill to the parking lot.

SUMMARY: The trail follows the river as closely as possible to the south end of the reserve, then loops out to the east, north, and west before rejoining the original trail again to return to the starting point.

THE WALK: Go to the southeast corner of the parking lot, that is, the corner closest to the Don Valley Parkway, and begin walking towards the river. Tend to the left to pass around a newly constructed pond, until you find the trail. The parks department has done a fair bit of terraforming: those little rocks were not always in the stream bed, many of the plants and trees did not start themselves, and the pond is a complete fabrication. This is one such effort that seems to be working out well. It will be interesting to watch as it matures over the years. You can pick up the trail is it enters the trees, just beyond the end of the pond and somewhat up the hill.

Further south, at the Forks of the Don, there is a plaque commemorating Charles Sauriol, who once lived there and spent much of his life documenting the early history of the river and fighting to preserve its natural beauty. The drive of the '50s to build expressways everywhere, combined with the real need for a transportation corridor to the heart of the city, resulted in the paving of much of the Don Valley. Through his books, other publications, and personal efforts, Charles

Sauriol did much to ensure that at least this much land was preserved for the enjoyment and instruction of future generations.

There are a number of trails through here, and there are no "right " ones. This description circumnavigates the reserve as much as possible, leaving exploration of the interior to individual initiative.

There are a number of unrecognized people who apparently love these trails, and without government payment or public acknowledgement they make small improvements to aid everyone's enjoyment. No attempts have been made to beautify the landscape, but when a substantial tree has fallen across the trail, the limbs have been cut away to leave it free and passable.

The first railway bridge is tall and old, built of I-beams riveted together into a very high structure crossing between the old riverbanks. The paint is peeling off rusting iron; it seems as though the bridge as well as the valley is being preserved as a historical artifact.

Just after the river crosses beneath the bridge, it forms a long pond. If there were any large fish in the river, some of them would live here. Look carefully; maybe some do.

The apartment buildings high up on the opposite bank are reminiscent of the high canyon caves of the American Southwest, home to native peoples thousands of years ago.

The river, the bank, and the trail all make a sharp left turn. At the second railway bridge, begin ascending a long, easy slope towards the rail line at the top. This track is in daily use, so look to the left, look to the right and cross carefully and quickly. Beyond the track is another hill to climb, considerably steeper this time. It leads to the top of the old riverbank, the "Toronto" level.

This is one of those parts of the walk where you can't just follow the trail, because it sometimes disappears over a cliff. There's usually a new loop formed. Take it even if the trail is still visible—undercutting of the bank by erosion could leave you walking on 30 centimetres of grass roots above a 15-metre drop.

The descent is moderately long, moderately steep, and sometimes a bit sticky in places. Ahead, the river meets a solid wall, and turns again sharply to the left.

The next railway bridge is more utilitarian than the other two, with just a couple of slabs of steel bolted together. It's sturdy and efficient and has a minimalist beauty. The trail goes down underneath the bridge and up the other side. Following that, there's a culverted stream.

When the trail forks, keep to the right.

The next climb is a long, steep one. Ignore the right fork and go straight ahead and up. If it's a slippery time, find things to grab and root steps for foot purchase. At the top, ignore the trail to the left and proceed straight ahead, walking away from the river. There's a deep ravine down to the right.

Coming out of the woods, follow the fence across to the right and up the other side, to where a trail leads to the right, following the opposite side of the ravine.

The edge of the river is marked by twin pines. Turn left along the bank, but not too close: this is one of those places where the trail goes flying from time to time. Take the right track at the fork and go on through groves of small trees.

At a crossroads where all the paths have been widened, take the one directly to the right, down the hill gently towards the river. Of necessity, you'll turn left and proceed along the edge. When the river jogs off to the right, the trail goes left, up a hill. At the split, go right.

The next part of the hill is not quite as gentle, and is much longer. Nevertheless it's easy enough walking. At the top the trail swings left. There's a path entering from the right, coming down from Wigmore Park.

A word of caution: local residents enjoy walking their dogs along here, and although most are very responsible about their stoop-and-scoop responsibilities, it pays to keep an eye on where you're stepping. At the next trail diversion continue ahead.

Keep an eye open for the apple trees, especially in late summer. You may find the fruit just a touch tart, but it presents a variety of flavours, and they're all juicy. A little later in the season this will smell like a fish and chips shop.

At the next fork, take the right side through a grove of pines and then to the lip of a ravine. Go right again.

Straight ahead the trail turns into a road, runs up a hill, and disappears into a residential neighbourhood. Make a sharp left down the grassy valley. Doesn't it look familiar, with the chain-link fence across the bottom? The loop is completed, and from now on the trail is a repeat, with a couple of detours.

Go down this gently sloping lawn towards the fence at the bottom, but angle a bit to the right end to connect up with the trail again.

At the entry to the woods take the branch to the right, past yet more apple trees, and then through the woodland. Another fork—take the right one. Cross a hump in the trail, and then go down again. Next, take a less well-defined trail off to the right, again uphill.

There's a bit of a mess here. There's one of those concrete portals that usually release little streams. Here there must have been a leak in the pipe, because there's the portal and then a row of disconnected pipe segments behind it. Go up to the top of the hole and turn left.

Take the trail down to the railway track, look both ways, then travel along the track to the left a few metres to the bridge, and descend the embankment down to the right to meet the trail. Ignore another trail going across the large field on the right side.

Back at the river again, remember that short steep hill you came down after crossing the railway tracks? Well, here's where you get to go up it again, towards the hemlocks. Cross the tracks, ignore the trail up to the right, and go straight.

Slowly the volume of traffic sound increases, as the trail approaches the bend in the river that parallels the expressway. A lowering sun makes this a high contrast, wicker-like maze of vines and branches and foliage.

The river finds itself straightened out once again, coming down from the Donalda Golf Course. Cross the open field towards the parking lot to the end of the walk.

GETTING BACK: For those taking public transport, simply retrace your steps. Go up the hill to Lawrence, then on up to Underhill, where you can cross at the traffic lights and take the westbound bus back to Eglinton Subway.

DON WALK 13
THE HILLY DON

DISTANCE: 6.75 kilometres

NOTE: Virtually all of this walk is on dirt trails, hence there's the usual warning about slipperiness in wet weather or winter thaws. There is one section where there is a long, steep climb followed by a passage where you'll be holding on to a chain-link fence for safety. There are a couple of passages along the lips of sharp drop-offs down to the river, and some others involve clambering over boggy little streams and up and down short, steep banks. Other than that, it's a fairly straightforward walk through riverine lands and some woods.

GETTING THERE BY PUBLIC TRANSIT: Take the Thorncliffe Park 81 bus from the Bloor/Danforth Subway at Pape to Thorncliffe Park Road, where it turns right. Get off the bus at a sign that reads: E. T. Seton Park, Central Don. At the bottom of the hill go left towards the parking lot. Just before the bridge, stop.

GETTING THERE BY AUTOMOBILE: Take the Don Valley Parkway and exit to Don Mills Road North. Keep to the right on the curve of the cloverleaf, and take the first exit on the right. Continue to an old concrete bridge on the left. Cross it and park in the parking lot.

Now by foot, cross the footbridge over the rail line at the end of the parking lot, turn sharp left down the ramp, follow the path to where it intersects a road, and turn sharply left to the other side of the bridge.

SUMMARY: The walk follows the west bank of the West Don up to the lands of York University, over a series of trails.

THE WALK: At the northwest corner of the bridge there's a path heading down parallel to the river. That's the corner at the upstream side of the bridge on the wild side of the river. Coming from the parking lot turn right, from the TTC turn left.

On the left are the usual bank-side willows, and up to the left is the side of the old riverbank, covered with a mixture of hardwood trees. Walk through a field liberally sprinkled with young trees and bushes until you enter a wood beneath the arch of a fallen willow limb.

The other side of the river all the way along will contain only mown grass and carefully planted trees. The paved bicycle trail passes along there, near or far, for most of the walk. It might as well be another world as far as this trail is concerned.

The first segment of trail is marked from time to time by the old posts used elsewhere to mark horse trails. They are about 2 metres high, 10 centimetres in diameter, brown below and orange for the top foot.

There's another horse trail sign just before the Overlea Boulevard Bridge, and some gentle up-and-downing for a while on the other side.

Follow a new stream up just a little way to a pair of pipeline signs. One is a white column of plastic about a metre high with a bright yellow top. Beside it is a post with a triangular sign on top. Just a short way beyond it, go down to the right to the stream and cross to the other side on stepping stones.

Turn sharply right along the stream back to the river. Turn left at the river, and avoid a small patch of bamboo. Now begins a climb up another hill to a plateau between a steep bank on the left and another down to the right. Judging by the moss and depth, this is an old path.

A stream comes down here, and you'll have to clamber over some slippery bits, jump down half a metre or so, follow a boggy sort of stream a short way ahead and then scramble up a bank on the left about a metre high. It's of the vertical persuasion, so find a plant or root assistant. The trail proceeds right along the edge here for a ways before drawing back a little.

Be careful at the place where the trail drops down beside the river; it's slippery at the best of times, and in cold months can become solid ice.

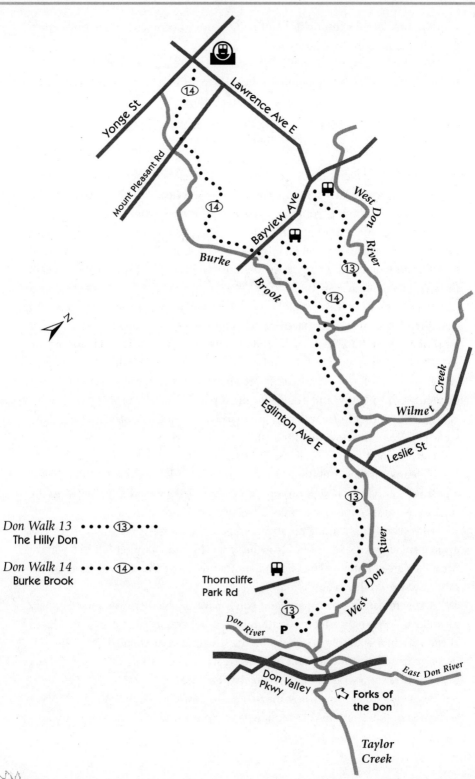

Don Walk 13 •••• ⑬ ••••
The Hilly Don

Don Walk 14 •••• ⑭ ••••
Burke Brook

Having reached a level stretch again, proceed with a few gentle up-and-downs to a wash coming down from the left. The original trail has been eroded, so you'll have to scramble up a mud bank here, and then there's another scramble up to the left to reconnect with the trail again.

When the trail forks, take the right one. As the trail eases back there's a fork to the left, but keep to the right. Climb over three fallen logs and then cross a short, boggy bit, often frozen and slippery in cold weather. The trail runs roughly midway between the river on the right and the old bank base on the left, and then it just sort of peters out. It's always safe to go to the river's edge and follow that.

Up ahead there is a descent from the top of the bank straight down to the water. It's mostly raw earth with a few small trees in it here and there. Most of it is loose and crumbly at the best of times, and very slippery when damp. You might be able to make it across, but on the other hand, once sliding downward there's nothing much to stop you until you're in the river. Carry on to a large old oak tree a metre or so from the riverbank, and then begin to angle up the hill to the top. This is not an especially easy climb. At the top there's an industrial yard bounded by a chain-link fence.

Continue along beside the fence across the top of the slide to the other side. Holding on to the fence for security is allowed. Once across, if you look around and down, there's a switch-back path, bordered by limbs and occasionally, pieces of plywood held in place by stakes. This will take you gently down to the bottom of the hill. The identity of the builders of this trail is unknown, but their work is greatly appreciated; there's been a lot of work done here.

Down at the floodplain level there's a path running parallel to the base of the hill. Follow it to the left. It leads to a paved path; follow it for a little. There's turf all around, and a formal fire circle off to the right.

Now look up, look way up. A Canadian Pacific Railway bridge crosses this whole valley. Walk on ahead beneath it. The paved path turns sharply to the right over a bridge. Continue straight ahead.

The red pine on the right is a sign to stick to the right-hand fork. This is now clearly a horse trail—it's deeply chewed up, and there are many hoof prints.

Follow the trail beneath the Eglinton Avenue Bridge. Near the top of the bridge on the other side there's a bus stop. The bus goes to the Eglinton Station on the Yonge Subway line.

Here the trail leads up a hill to an open park. Continue along the right side, towards a wood. As the path approaches a bridge, the main trail goes off to the right through a grove of mature hemlocks. Take a sharp left, and go down past the suspension footbridge and up the little hill ahead. Suspension bridges are not common around here.

At the top of the hill, walk across a park into bushes and small trees on the other side. They descend to a paved pathway.

Just a little way to the right there's a washroom, open half the year. Follow the paved path along as it curves slowly up to the left. The path forks, with a smaller paved path going off to the right down to a bridge.

About halfway along the curve, there's a trail off to the right, descending rapidly to the river. Although it is steep, there are lots of roots forming steps, and it is in fact a fairly easy descent. At the river, continue on past the end of a chain-link fence.

A spur comes down from the bank to the left and continues right to the river, where it is cut off sharply. The trail mounts it right at the sharp edge, a bit uncomfortably close; it's easier and safer to walk a short way to the left.

Looking over at the river you may notice that it's not the West Don River anymore. It is in fact a tributary called Burke Brook, flowing down through Sherwood and other parks from near Yonge and Lawrence Avenues. But that's another walk and another story (Don Walk 14: Burke Brook). It flows into the West Don just a little way down from the bridge.

The bridge carries a road down from up to the left somewhere, across this valley beside the river to a parking lot on the other side. Head for that parking lot, cutting across the valley without following the road if you like.

At the parking lot there's another road crossing at right angles, coming down from Sunnybrook Hospital up to the left and going over a bridge to the road from the horse barns there. Right beside the bridge, take the trail going down beside the river. People walk their dogs along here: mind your step.

When you enter the grounds of the Glendon Campus of York University, up to the left is a sports field with soccer goals and a baseball cage. Walk along an old dirt road between the edge of the field and the river at an intermediate level.

At another old footbridge, the road turns up to the left. Follow it along the north side of the field, up towards the university buildings.

Continue on the paved road that runs on up a hill, then take the old roadway running gently up towards the top of the bank. Up top is the original Glendon Hall Mansion the campus is named for.

At the top of the road, curve around to the right, past the end of the red brick residences to a paved path. Head for the building with a gold figure inscribed on it. Turn a bit left, walk under an enclosed walkway and on to a roadway. Continue on the roadway to the left, past the booth and to the left towards Bayview

Avenue, now both visible and audible. This will be the end of peace and quiet until your next walk.

GETTING BACK: Right at the street entrance (Lawrence Avenue), there's a bus stop. Catch the 124 bus along Lawrence Avenue to the Lawrence Subway Station. For those who left a car at the beginning, take the subway down to Bloor, then east to Pape. Follow the Getting There by Public Transit directions at the beginning. If you have the time and the energy, it's also possible to go back to the bridge leading to the stables on the other side, and follow the paved path south to the beginning.

DON WALK 14
BURKE BROOK

DISTANCE: 5.5 kilometres
NOTE: There is only one difficult section—descending from Bayview Avenue. More than half of the first bit is through Alexander Muir Gardens and Sherwood Park, on well-maintained paths. There is a section on less well cared for but very passable trails beside the Burke Brook itself. There are a number of short wet sections, and one short but slippery, especially boggy bit.
GETTING THERE BY PUBLIC TRANSPORT: Take the Yonge Subway to Lawrence Station and go to the south exit on the east side.
GETTING THERE BY AUTOMOBILE: There is public parking two blocks north of Lawrence, off Yonge on the east side. Look for the large green "P" in a circle. Walk south to the subway exit on the northeast corner of Yonge and Lawrence.
SUMMARY: The walk follows local park paths two blocks south to the entrance to Alexander Muir Gardens, and then follows paths and trails east through the ravine, almost to the West Don, then north and west into the Sunnybrook Hospital complex to a bus stop. The bus will bring you back to the beginning of the walk at Lawrence and Yonge.
THE WALK: Cross Lawrence Avenue south past the library, to a path leading down through the park. Walk on past the playground and up the steps on the other side. Cross Lympstone Avenue, and continue along the path across the east side of the park. From the valley configuration it's reasonable to assume that this was the location of one of Toronto's many buried streams, since it runs right down to the Burke Brook Ravine.

Cross another street and begin the descent into the Alexander Muir Gardens, down the crushed redbrick path. This a most beautiful formal garden. You'll be through it in a moment, however, if time is not a consideration and if the season is right, it's well worth your attention.

Continue to follow the redbrick path to a paved roadway. Cross this and turn left on to the paths on the other side.

First on the left are tennis courts, followed closely by a bowling green. On the right, Burke Brook emerges from the underworld through a steel-barred concrete portal. At this stage it's hardly a brook, barely a streamlet in fact; but give it time, and the right underworld connections. It's been buried since its beginnings, and even now is tightly controlled between vertical banks of concrete blocks, topped by sloping banks of stone.

At the end of the paved roadway there's a small parking lot, and at the far end of that there's a woodchip path continuing along parallel to the brook.

Beyond the Mount Pleasant Road Bridge the path leads up to a street. But before that, there's another path leading down to the right beside the stream. The stream had disappeared into a portal on the other side of Bayview and now reappears from another on this side.

At the end of this little valley the brook does its habitual disappearing act, and the path goes over Blythwood Road. On the other side, in Sherwood Park, Burke Brook reemerges, and the path splits to go down both sides. Take an alternate path going up to the left into a wood. There is a sign, Nature Trail. The path now follows the edge of the park up near the rim.

For anyone interested in tree identification, here's a challenge. Forget the sugar maple and red oak and beech—there are lots of those. Can you find the basswood, ironwood, elm, eastern cottonwood, silver maple, linden, white ash or black cherry?

Some of this may well be original forest. Judging from the number of people and dogs often present here, this is very much a community place to walk the pet and stop to talk with friends and neighbours. Unfortunately, both kids and dogs should be kept on a leash in this park, as the banks have been scrubbed bare. Not only do we have to place wild animals in zoos for their own protection, but we now have to fence off trees too. It's a pity, but probably inevitable if the habitat is to be preserved.

The only thing covering the gravel on these banks is a little soil, composted from leaf mould over the years. When this very thin cover is scraped off by feet, dogs, or a mountain bike's knobby tires, there's nothing much to keep the whole thing from sliding down into the valley. This is always a potential problem when delicate natural conditions occur in the middle of a heavily used urban area, and will only become more problematic with time as the population grows. Closing trails, and perhaps even closing whole sections of the park, may be the best hope of maintaining some of the original habitat.

Take a fork down towards the top of a flight of steps, and turn left just before reaching them. Continue to an extensive stretch of boardwalk leading over a section of hillside. This stretch is quite boggy and very susceptible to damage, not to mention being slippery and wet.

Descend now to where the creek flows beneath the path, through a large culvert. Continue up the hill to the avenue.

On the other side of Bayview there are two ways back down to the stream, but you want to end up on the north (left) side. On the south side there's sort of a path down an eroded gulch, leading over the portal where the stream emerges.

On the north side of the stream there is a small ravine running down to the creek, with a chain-link fence beside it. The easiest way down is by holding onto the fence; it's steep, and this way too can be slippery at times.

At the bottom follow the path that leads downstream. It's a clear path, a good path, but not a Sherwood Park path. Judging by the size of some of the trees, this is probably a remnant of the original forest. In addition, there's lots of younger growth, ensuring a healthy succession process.

This area is instructive about what a difference ease of access makes to an environment. This section of Burke Brook is a little tricky to get to. With no signage and no community involvement, it's been left to fend for itself. It is unimproved—when trees land, they lie where they fall. When erosion changes the course of the stream, it follows its new path.

This place is perhaps not pretty, but it's beautiful. It's not so convenient, but it's restful. It feeds the soul and restores equanimity. There is a need for both kinds of park, and it is to be hoped that there will continue to be a place for retreats such as this in Toronto in years to come.

Upon entering a field, the trail parts company with the brook. It continues on down to the right and flows into the West Don River.

Walk to the left to skirt a small wetland, complete with boggy soil, wetland plants and small ponds of open water. It's a great place for kids to explore. If they've survived the constraints of Sherwood Park and the boggy wildness of the last stretch, they deserve the chance to run, yell, fall, get dirty and do those things which so delighted adults lo, those many years ago.

Follow the edge of the wetland until eventually you come to a wooded hillside. Walk to a parking lot. Turn left and climb the road up a long, long, long hill. There's a deep and dark hemlock forest up the bank on the left side. Hemlocks can survive the cooler north slope better than the other trees.

Follow the road through the complex of hospital buildings to the bus stop.

GETTING BACK: The 124 bus will take you to the Lawrence Subway Station.

INTERLUDE 4
ANTS

A worker ant is less than one millionth the size of a worker human, but collectively, ants rival humans as the dominant organisms on the planet. When you lean on a tree almost anywhere, the first creature to crawl across your pinkie will probably be an ant. Walk along a sidewalk in the heart of downtown, or beside a stream or a field in the country, and count the different kinds of small critters you see: the ants will come up winners every time.

It's been calculated very conservatively that the number of individual ants on the Earth's surface could be about ten thousand trillion. Individual ants weigh on average between 1 to 5 milligrams, so taken all together, all the ants in the world weigh about the same as all the humans. But because of their smaller size, ants have better penetration of the environment, which means they go and live in places we can't, won't or don't.

In this part of the world they probably excavate about as much soil as earthworms, which is a lot. Turning over and aerating the soil is vital to plant growth. They're also responsible for dispersal of up to a third of herbaceous plant species, and those two activities alone are important in maintaining all life on earth.

Ants develop through four stages: egg, larva (wormlike, eating and growing), pupa (rest and body change), and adult. There are three adult forms: queens, males and workers. Sometimes workers may be of two or three sizes, with specialized functions. For instance, large workers may be soldiers or guards.

Once a year winged males and females emerge from the colony and mate—often in flight. Then the males die and the females establish new colonies.

The ants' most effective survival tool is social organization.

Social insects evolved during Cretaceous times, 140 to 65 million years before the birth of Karl Marx. The successful social insects with the most complex societies share three characteristics: adults care for the young; two or more generations live together in the same nest; and members of each colony are divided into a reproductive "royal" caste, and a non-reproductive "worker" caste.

Highly social insects such as ants and termites can out-compete solitary insects for the most desirable nest sites because of increased labour efficiency. Who would you rather have build your car: a single worker having a bad day, or a whole bunch, only a couple of whom are having a bad day?

Social insects such as ants have a much stronger tendency to self-sacrifice than do solitary insects. Their genes are colony genes, and will survive and be handed down to succeeding generations whether or not the individual survives.

Self-sacrificial, colonial socialism really works under some circumstances. Marx just applied his concept to the wrong species.

The queen is in all ways the heart of the colony, but the path to that position is fraught with danger. For every queen that founds a colony, hundreds or even thousands die. If colonies typically last five years (until the queen dies), and if only one virgin queen from five colonies will successfully start a colony each year, and if a typical colony releases 100 virgin queens a year, then only one in 500 has a chance of survival. Males, on the other hand, have zero chance of a long life—they die hours after leaving the nest. Workers just keep on working until something eats them or they wear out.

The queen begins her reign as a highly versatile, self-reliant adult. She starts with wings, but scrapes them off after the nuptial flight to allow greater mobility. She then digs a nest and lays eggs. After they hatch she gathers food to feed her daughters' grub-like, helpless forms over a period of weeks or months. She protects them during this and the pupa stage, until finally they hatch into adult workers. From this moment onward they look after her, and she becomes an egg-laying machine for the rest of her life. As long as she survives, the colony organism survives. Some species maintain their colony's existence even longer by allowing for multiple queens.

Males and reproductive females are born by choice of the queen, only after the colony is well established, and just before mating season.

Just as in a human family or any type of social organization, on-going, intensive communication is an imperative of success. The ants' antennae operate something like our noses—they can use them to detect different chemical substances in the air or on the ground. They come equipped with a number of specialized glands at both ends that secrete fluids that carry their own unique identifiers. They can mix and order four or five substances in different combinations to convey different meanings.

They can mark territory, much as dogs and many other mammals do, and when they find food, they can lay a trail back to the nest to guide others. They may touch a nestmate with two antennae or offer a drop of the food to taste and convince, if it's in liquid form.

A type of weaver ant releases four types of chemical. They diffuse through the air at different rates and are detected at different concentrations, so others become aware of them in progressive stages. The first arouses, something like a jolt of caffeine. The second alarms, like an ambulance siren. The third one attracts the recipients closer to the source and stimulates them to bite any foreign object. The last one has an effect that makes road rage seem like mild irritation.

But a full working vocabulary needs more than just these techniques to be effective, so the preferred mode of communication is through pheromones. It's estimated that ant species may use between ten and twenty chemical "words" and "phrases," each conveying a distinct but very general meaning.

Some kinds of ants are farmers, that tend and "milk" aphids. The term "milk" is a euphemism. Aphids feed on plant juices, and what they don't need themselves, about 90 percent sugars, they exude in droplets from the end of their bodies farthest from the head. Entomologists call this stuff honeydew. Many ants love honeydew, so much in fact that they will actually protect the aphids. Ant wars have been fought over the question of who owns an aphid. The relationship is a perfect example of symbiosis in nature. The aphids get protection, even nurturing sometimes, and the ants get fed.

Within the family *Formicidae* (ants), there are at least twenty-five genera occurring in Ontario. If you look closely and keep notes, odds are you'll be able to spot most of them. Start in your own backyard or any open bit of land.

CHAPTER 5

THE HIGHLAND CREEK
WATERSHED

Both of Highland Creek's two main branches, Highland Creek and West Highland Creek, begin their lives far south of the bigger watercourses, well within the city limits. A search for the headwaters would lead you to somebody's backyard.

It's possible to walk beside the main creek from Markham Road and Progress Avenue right down to Lake Ontario, if you have time and stamina. You might need a pair of rubber boots in a couple of places, plus a long day's time, but it can be done. You would be passing through undeveloped parkland for at least half the distance, and there are trails off the paved path for much of the remainder. West Highland Creek has a couple of stretches good for walking, but the Scarborough Golf and Country Club sits right across the middle portion, and it blocks any attempt to remain beside the stream.

If you think of these valleys as being perhaps nine or ten thousand years old, you're probably right. You might then assume that the ground you're walking on beside a stream might be of a similar age. It isn't necessarily so.

In the Morningside Park area, between Military Trail and Morningside Avenue, there are a number of structures in the creek bed. In addition to the usual presence of limestone blocks or gabion baskets to control erosion, there are places where huge slabs of limestone have been set into the creek bottom itself, sloping up front to back and filled in behind with gravel. They were constructed in the late '90s to protect sewer pipes running beneath the creek bed. One might ask why a sewer pipe would be laid so close to the bottom of the creek as to need this protection. The answer is, it wasn't.

When the sewers were laid, there was lots of creek bed above them. That bed, composed of sand and gravel, has been eroded, perhaps as much as 6 or 7 metres within the memorable past. The gravel we walk on today beside the stream was buried deeply not so many years ago.

Another artifact attesting to the speed of erosion may be seen across the stream from a public washroom (Highland Walk 2). There's an old footbridge there, lying well back from the present stream, in what seems like a funny sort of place to build a bridge. In fact, when it was built, it spanned the creek. The creek moved—it moved a lot, and now there's a bridge with no stream to cross.

Geological change can be slow. It usually is, but when it comes to these watersheds in the old gravel beds around Toronto, it can also be surprisingly fast. More about this when we consider Hurricane Hazel.

Many of the descriptions of the Rouge in the next chapter will apply to Highland Creek as well, especially those referring to the diversity of flora and fauna. The fact that the watershed is not directly connected to the much larger Rouge except by a hydro corridor doesn't seem to have stopped wildlife from migrating. Most years there will be deer in Morningside Park, and it's possible to bump into any of the other usual mammals as well.

After the last ice age, both mastodons and mammoths roamed this land. Not just Highland Creek, of course, but a goodly section of the continent. Bones of both have been found in Indiana in the same geological formations that exist here, and a skeleton unearthed at Wellandport on the Niagara Peninsula is now in the Royal Ontario Museum. Bones of both beasts are still discovered from time to time near the old Lake Iroquois shoreline. These proto-elephants seem to have disappeared about six thousand years ago, when the temperature suddenly increased.

There were settlers here long before beaver hats became popular in Europe, or the potato famine forced people to leave Ireland. Archaeologists have found the remains of campsites that have been carbon-dated back nine thousand years.

Much more recently, the remains of a village were found on a 4-hectare site close to where Brimley Road crosses West Highland Creek. Carbon dating indicates it was occupied around 1250 A.D. Along with the usual artifacts, spear and arrow heads, clay pipes and pottery shards were found close by, as well as a large ossuary—the people who used to live here in that time often buried their dead in large communal graves.

Settlements were not maintained over long periods of time. A good portion of the people's diet was composed of corn, squash and beans, which provided much of their nutritional requirements. But the corn especially depleted the soil quite quickly.

The community used up suitable firewood within easy carrying distance of the settlement, and the garbage midden became ever larger. And so at some time, when life's daily chores became too burdensome, the tribe would pick up and move on, leaving the forest to reclaim the land and heal its wounds.

Some time just before the coming of the French, the resident tribes completed a slow migration from around Lake Ontario, north to Lake Simcoe and Georgian Bay. This took them further away from marauding Iroquois, and in addition the soil was lighter in texture than the heavy clays closer to the lake, and therefore easier to work with wooden tools.

Scarborough Township, of which Highland Creek Watershed formed a goodly part, was the scene of the first great land speculation in this part of the world. New settlers accepted a small grant of land in York, or north along Yonge Street, but as a further inducement or reward many asked for, and were granted, acreages in Scarborough. Others bought theirs. Sizes might range from as little as 120 hectares up to as much as 1,000 hectares. Some individuals actually went out and cut down trees to create a farm, but most simply held title until they could sell the land at a profit.

The first-known settler in the area was a Scot named David Thomson, who acquired a piece of land near today's Scarborough General Hospital. He worked at his stonemason's trade in York much of the time, but whenever he could, he hiked out to his piece of woodland to chop down trees. He built a cabin, cleared a little land and moved his wife and four children out to their new home. While he laboured in town, his wife, Mary, looked after the kids, planted and cultivated some crops, made tallow candles, wove cloth and made clothes, fed the livestock, carried water and cooked. During much of the time she was pregnant. David came out whenever he could, but Mary often lived alone with the children for weeks at a time, during all seasons. Once she had to use an axe to stop a bear from carrying off the family pig. By the time they had produced a couple more children, they had created a viable little farm in the forest.

In the winter of 1804, another early settler, William Connel, drove his sled to Kingston along tracks through the forest, bought millstones, and, paying for them with a "span of colts," drove back to Highland Creek and built the first of many mills on the stream.

David and Mary and William were typical of many of the early settlers, something to keep in mind as we stand complaining about having to wait ten minutes for a bus.

While walking one of the trails described here, stop for a moment, look out over the valley, and imagine.

NORTH LOOP

DISTANCE: 4 kilometres

NOTE: This route follows paved paths, trails and no trails; there are some wet, boggy sections and some substantial hills.

GETTING THERE BY PUBLIC TRANSIT: Take the Bloor/Danforth Subway east to Kennedy Station and the 116 Morningside bus to the bottom of the hill where Morningside crosses Highland Creek. Cross the road and walk down the paved path on the left side of the roadway to the parking lot.

GETTING THERE BY AUTOMOBILE: Drive north on Morningside Avenue from Lawrence Avenue, or south from Ellesmere Road to the entrance, signed Morningside Park, Highland Creek, just north of the creek on the west side of the road. Drive down to the parking lot.

SUMMARY: From the second parking lot, the walk loops out around "the mountain," descending to the flats and following the base of "the mountain" around to intersect the road. It then follows the road past a third parking lot down to the river, keeping to the left on a gravelled path, and back to the start.

THE WALK: Just at the entrance back beside Morningside Avenue is all that remains of a beaver pond. One look around to the north and you can tell by the number of dead trees that there has been extensive flooding in earlier times. Every few years a pair of beaver come this way and go about patching up the dam, knocking down a few aspens for the winter. They then come out to this corner and find out where all the water goes—right through these two culverts, down under the road here to the river. Well, it's pretty obvious even to a beaver that a little mud and a few sticks shoved in that culvert is just going to solve everything. And then the water rises . . . and rises. Then one frosty winter morning somebody comes driving along here and finds out that when the dam overflows the water comes right out here on the road and gives it a nice coating of smooth, slippery ice.

The people at the parks department have learned about beaver over the years, so when they see that dam getting higher than it ought to, the beaver are live-trapped and helped to emigrate. A good big hole is dug out of the dam, the pond disappears, and life goes on.

(Is it really necessary to deport the beaver? Be assured that every time a hole is punched in a beaver dam, no matter how big, it's going to be patched back up in almost no time at all. Yes, the beaver have to go.)

At the far side of the parking lot, across a footbridge, is a washroom open all year. Might as well check in while there's an opportunity. Walk past the parking lot to the right and on down the road. Around to the left there's another parking lot. Just past the beginning, there's a trail heading off to the right to the edge of a wood. The entrance is marked by a green and white sign standing up on a long green pole, and three brown posts sticking up about a metre above the ground.

The trail mounts a little rise, tends to the right and forks in three directions; take the one to the right. It quickly dives down towards some vine-laden trees, with the bog of the old beaver pond to the right.

At the next fork, go right. In time the trail leads up a long, high hill.

Coming to a ridge, turn right, up another trail following the ridge line. The trail, with all its bumps and hollows, is gently climbing towards the top of the old riverbank at the level of today's city.

Because of its steepness this trail can be slippery at times, especially when covered with wet leaves or melting snow. Best to watch your footing.

At the top is a tableland covered by trees. There are a lot of birch trees here, both fallen and standing. There's a reason for that. When an area is burned or slash cut so that the soil is exposed, all tree species contribute seeds to get things started again. Some trees, such as paper birch, are very fast off the mark, and grow higher and faster than anything else. However the slower-growing, shade-loving beech, maple and oak just keep on coming, and eventually pass the birches. The birches don't thrive in shade, so they die and fall down.

In a grove of sumac there's a huge mass of horsetails growing. Horsetails are plants consisting mainly of a dark green shoot with whitish joints and hairs for leaves; they are quite striking and primitive looking.

Further along is a grove of mostly young white pines. They have grown up together, possibly from an original planting or reforestation effort. Like the birch,

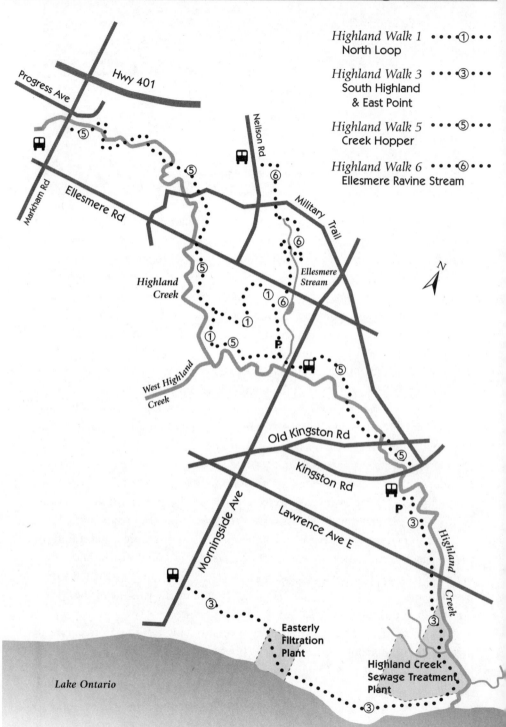

Highland Walk 1 •••①•••
North Loop

Highland Walk 3 •••③•••
South Highland
& East Point

Highland Walk 5 •••⑤•••
Creek Hopper

Highland Walk 6 •••⑥•••
Ellesmere Ravine Stream

114

they don't grow in the shade, so a white pine forest can never duplicate itself without the intervention of fire, man, or some other disaster. Again, the shade-tolerant maple, oak and beech will eventually take over.

At the first fork continue on straight ahead, at the second turn right. At the edge of the trees turn left along the edge of the forest. Sometimes there's a path through here and sometimes there isn't. Either way, continue parallel to Ellesmere Road.

At end of the pine grove and the beginning of turf in front of apartment buildings, turn left to follow the tree line down behind the buildings. There's a black chain-link fence to follow closely here, around to the right, until you reach a sharp jog. To your left there's a faintly discernible path, marked by a grey surveyor's stake about a metre high with a yellow top. Turn left here and keep walking till you come to the lip of a ravine. Turn left.

At any time of the year, but especially in winter, if you have been moving quietly there's always a possibility of startling a pair of deer in here. In fact, that could happen anyplace in the Highland Creek Watershed.

At last the trail moves to the left, away from the lip of the bank, and in a few moments it joins the trail you followed up here. For the next little while then you'll be retracing your steps. That's okay, things always look different from the other side.

At the first fork keep to the right, and at the next one leave this old trail and take the right one down to the valley below.

At the bottom, turn back almost 180 degrees and follow the base of the hill back the other way. Eventually you'll circumnavigate this flatland and return to the roadway.

Don't look for a trail along here; there isn't one. You'll have to pick your way in places. This is mostly open woodland, but as with all natural woodlands trees lie where they fall, and the tendency for trees dying on a hill is to fall downwards, right across the direction of travel.

Finally the bank begins to turn to the left. Follow it around to reach the road and turn right.

In the cold months, any place along here is a good place to feed chickadees. Choose a place that has trees right up beside the road, so that the birds have a place close by to perch and survey the scene. Then put some seed in your hand, stretch it out a little ways, stand very still, and wait. Chickadee feeding is a common pastime along here, and the birds have grown used to the possibility of a free handout. If you're walking through brush or a grove of young trees anywhere in the neighbourhood, and there's a flock of chickadees passing by, it's not at all uncommon for one to perch a short ways away and wait expectantly.

Past the parking lot the paved road becomes a gravel path, and leads directly ahead towards Highland Creek. This field is well mown and set up for picnics, complete with tables and fire stands. There's even another washroom, closed in the freezing months, unfortunately.

Follow the path to the left, along the long pile of rocks beside the creek if you like, then clamber up to the gravel path roughly paralleling it.

When the creek turns sharply left, the one path becomes many. Take the one meandering along through groves of sumac. At the footbridge turn left, and follow this new paved path beside the stream.

Off to the left, parkland appears, and up ahead is the year-round washroom. Continue on past it and the parking lot out towards Morningside Road.

GETTING BACK: Go to the bus stop just to the left of the roadway where it meets Morningside, and wait for the 116 Morningside bus, which travels back to the Kennedy Station on the Bloor/Danforth Subway.

HIGHLAND WALK 2
WEST HIGHLAND LOOP

DISTANCE: 3 kilometres or 6 kilometres

NOTE: The success of this whole walk depends upon crossing the creek at a ford. In high water, don't even try it. In winter, ice on the stones makes it treacherous. In warm weather, bare feet will get you across. Some of the trail is on paved or gravelled roads, and most of the rest is fairly easy walking.

GETTING THERE BY PUBLIC TRANSIT: Take the Bloor/Danforth Subway east to Kennedy Station. Take the 116 Morningside bus to the bottom of the hill where Morningside crosses Highland Creek, at the main entrance to Morningside Park. Cross the road and walk down the paved path on the left side of the roadway to the parking lot.

GETTING THERE BY AUTOMOBILE: Drive north on Morningside Avenue from Lawrence, or south from Ellesmere Road to the entrance signed Morningside Park, Highland Creek, just north of the creek on the west side of the road.

SUMMARY: This walk leads from Morningside parking lot, north along Highland Creek to a ford just north of the West Highland Creek confluence, then up West Highland Creek and an unnamed tributary to Lawrence Avenue. Alternative return is possible along a paved path on the south side of West Highland Creek, looping back to the Morningside parking lot.

THE WALK: First of all, note that there is a year-round washroom at the far side of the parking lot. Lord knows when you'll see another.

From the west (left) end of the parking lot, turn right down the paved path running parallel to the river. Cross the bridge over the little stream coming in from the left. The playing field is huge and well groomed, and there are abundant picnic facilities. Follow the path along past an inward bow of the creek.

Just before the bridge, up to the right you can see the result of water seeping through the sand and gravel forming this high bank. It has caused the face of the hill to slide off, taking full-grown trees, roots and all, along with it.

Leave the bridge and the paved path leading off to the left, and follow the wider, older path leading to the right, a little further from the creek, down through the trees.

Ahead there's been extensive stone fill put in on this side of the creek. Beyond that again, humongous blocks of limestone have been placed in the creek itself, and that's where you're headed. Walk along beside the rocks to the end of the fill, and then clamber up to the top of a long line of big limestone chunks piled along this bank. Just at this juncture is the easiest place to climb down to the creek level, and turn right to the large stones spanning the creek bed. This is the ford described in the introduction, and with a little care you'll be able to cross the river with most-ly dry feet. A stick or staff helps. If conditions are not suitable for crossing, consider one of the other walks, such as Highland Walks 1 or 6.

Go up the bank on the other side and turn left. In front is what looks like a section of bridge, rising from nowhere in particular to a concrete support placing it a short distance above the ground, also in the middle of nowhere. This bridge did cross the creek, until the creek moved away. The speed at which this, or any stream, can change its course is enough to break an engineer's heart.

Keep to the left of the whole mess, and step up a small bank to a slightly higher level where the old roadway comes down. Take the fork leading down beside the water. The path isn't always clear, but since it follows the stream it's easy enough to pick up again if lost.

Highland Creek makes a sharp left turn and stumbles down a series of rapids. Around to the left there's a pile of rocks and a sewer cover. Go straight over to the vertical bank and clamber up it by holding on to roots and shrubs and moving your feet really fast. You can follow the water around to the left—there's a short stretch literally right at the water's edge, but it can be slippery.

After reaching the top of the rock pile, go inland just a little, and then follow the path to the left to a large culvert, mostly above ground, carrying a little stream down to the creek.

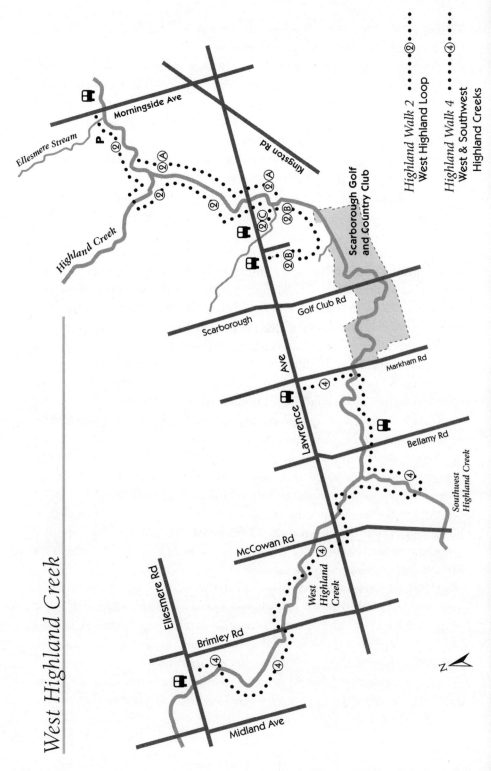

West Highland Creek

Morningside Ave

Ellesmere Stream

Highland Creek

Kingston Rd

P

2
Ⓐ
2
2
2
2Ⓒ
2Ⓐ
2Ⓑ
2Ⓑ

Scarborough Golf and Country Club

Scarborough

Golf Club Rd

Markham Rd

Lawrence Ave

4

Bellamy Rd

4

Southwest Highland Creek

McCowan Rd

4

West Highland Creek

Ellesmere Rd

Brimley Rd

4

4

Midland Ave

N

Highland Walk 2
West Highland Loop
②

Highland Walk 4
West & Southwest
Highland Creeks
④

At the next fork, bear on straight ahead. The trail curves slowly around to the right, and eventually it comes out to a stream bank. This is West Highland Creek, and down to the left it joins up with its other half to form the united Highland Creek. After flowing through some of the remnants of the original Carolinian forest, eventually it reaches Lake Ontario. That's another walk, though, Highland Walk 3.

There's a well-used path going up to the right into the forest on the hillside; however, stick more to the creek side and follow it along upstream.

After passing a low steel weir across the creek, there's a vertical bank directly across the path. Moving a short way to the right, you'll find a short scramble path up to the top. Keep to the trail that goes straight ahead, parallel to the creek. Now on your right there's a long, skinny pond running parallel to the trail.

At the grove of white cedars, take the fork leading straight ahead. At the end of the pond, the trail climbs and leads along a little spur between lower land on left and right. When the path splits, follow the one going down to the left, then around a curve to the right again as it follows the base of the hill.

Just past the Lawrence Avenue Bridge there's a sign warning off skiers and toboggan riders and the like.

As the creek swings around to the right, the trail comes to a concrete structure in the river. It looks as if a concrete-bottomed spillway was built, and then the creek worked its way underneath. There's now a very fast and dangerous-looking fall of water beneath it. It's potentially deadly dangerous to children and possibly even adults. A little further up there's a small weir.

The trail comes to a place where a stream comes down from the right to join the creek. The creek makes a sharp turn, and there's a paved path crossing it on a bridge. At this point there are three options. Option A: It's easy to find a ford across the stream if you go up it a little ways, then cross over and follow the paved path beside the creek back to the parking lot. Option B: Follow the paved path along the West Humber until you come to Cedar Ridge Park, then walk for a few minutes through suburban streets to Lawrence Avenue. Option C: Follow the path up along this stream to Lawrence Avenue.

Option A: Walk up the unnamed tributary a little way, to an island in the middle. Climb down a groove in the bank, over to the stream, and step across to the island. There are stepping stones over to the far side, and there's a tree root to hold on to on as you scramble to the top.

If this particular ford is not do-able for any reason, there are others; just go upstream a little further, cross, then walk back down here.

Cross over West Highland Creek on the footbridge, and keep to the path as it curves to the right and starts up a hill. Keep to the paved path. Just past the

Lawrence Avenue Bridge is a trail to the left, going down to the creek, where the trail continues beside the bank.

In time you'll have to climb the small ridge you came down earlier. The trail curves away from the water, mounts a rise, and suddenly you're back on the path.

Sooner than you might expect, you're at the convergence of the Highland and West Highland Creeks again. Way up to the right there's a high, very steep and eroded slope. There's a sign way up at the top facing this way, and if you were to climb up close enough to read it you could see, Danger, Do Not Climb on Slopes. The mind truly boggles!

Crossing the bridge on the paved path, keep following it along beside the river. When you get up the hill past the phragmites, cut across the greensward towards the washroom and then to the Morningside parking lot. This completes Option A.

Option B: After crossing the little stream, go up to the paved path and turn right just before the bridge. It's flat and open here, with the river to your left. In time you come to another footbridge. Continue along a path to the right, still on this side of the river. There's a guardrail in one spot, although this could hardly be considered a dangerous walk.

In time you'll encounter a series of switchbacks, as the trail gently mounts the old riverbank. The path is well maintained, with logs along the edges to prevent slipping. As you get higher, there are also railings to hold on to.

At a branching of the ways go left and then left again up to the top of the bank. There's a house just to the right and a chain-link fence along the edge of the bank to the left. That's welcome, because it's a long drop down to the river.

Once at the top, you're rewarded by being allowed to go down again. It's a long gentle descent to the edge of a long gully, filled with big old trees, gorgeous in the fall. Continue up again along the edge of the gully.

The hairpin to the right is followed by a turn to the left and behold, you're in a parking lot. Walk over to the gate, where there's a sign telling you that you're exiting from Cedar Ridge Creative Centre.

Start north on Tingle Crescent to Confederation Drive, jog a little left to Summerbridge, turn right on Marcell Street to Susan, and left on Susan, past the school to Lawrence.

GETTING BACK (A & B): If travelling by public transport, cross Lawrence (carefully) and catch the 54 bus to Lawrence East Station on the LRT. If using a car, go back to Kennedy Station and then catch the 116 bus to Morningside.

Option C: Turning right up the stream, follow what is almost a road. Further on there's a manmade waterfall, very pretty, especially in the leafy months. Unfortunately it's a hard scramble down the solid embankments to get a good view. Not dangerous, just difficult. The water falls out of a concrete trough above, over three tiers down to the pond below. In warm times, the concrete is covered by green moss and surrounded by a host of plants of all kinds.

Eventually all good things must end, and this stream soon dives beneath Lawrence Avenue into one of those concrete portals guarded by steel bars. The path leads up a gentle incline towards the street. Just to the right, Orton Road, coming down from the north, joins Lawrence and there are traffic lights. Go to the corner.

GETTING BACK (C): Cross the road, go to the bus shelter, and take the westbound 54A bus to the Lawrence East Station on the LRT subway extension. Those who drove should stay on the south side of Lawrence and take the eastbound 54A bus to Morningside, where you transfer to the southbound 116 bus to the park entrance.

SOUTH HIGHLAND & EAST POINT

DISTANCE: 7 kilometres

NOTE: This whole trail is easy walking, without any steep hills or especially wet stretches. Trails are always easily visible and usually fairly wide. There is no danger as long as you keep to the posted trail along the bluffs. About half of this trail is through open grassland, unlike many of the others. In May, June and July, make sure to take the bug spray.

GETTING THERE BY PUBLIC TRANSPORT: Take the Bloor/Danforth Subway to Kennedy Station, then the 86A Scarborough East bus to the first stop east of the second bridge. The first bridge crosses the railway line, the second, Highland Creek. This stop is just before the bus turns off Kingston Road to go to Highway 2 and Old Kingston Road. Follow the roadway curving down into the valley.

GETTING THERE BY AUTOMOBILE: During ice-free months, drive east on Kingston Road to the turnoff to Highway 2. Start the turn but almost immediately make a right turn down the hill. Follow the road over the bridge to the parking lot.

In winter months the road down into the park is closed. The easiest way to access the park during these months is to drive to the Kennedy Subway Station at Eglinton and Kennedy Road, and park in the TTC parking lot.

SUMMARY: This walk follows close to Highland Creek, down to the GO railway tracks. It then crosses a bridge beside the creek and proceeds west, parallel to the GO line, around the Highland Creek Sewage Treatment Plant, to a road. From there the trail follows the bluffs to the Easterly Filtration Plant, along a road, a right-of-way beside the GO line, and then along a trail to Morningside Road.

THE WALK: Those who came by TTC will continue down the road and across a bridge over the creek. Just after crossing the bridge, take the little trail down to the left, and follow along beside the water. There are picnic facilities everywhere.

Both creek and trail move around to the right to the parking lot, where those who drove here can begin their walk. It's okay, you haven't missed anything too exciting.

Up on the other side of the parking lot there's a warm-weather washroom.

Until the mid '90s the only way down to the lake was by foot. It was a challenging walk, with a couple of very steep climbs and much winding back and forth. The walk will follow this old original trail as often as possible, omitting a couple of the steep hills. Considerable effort has been made to make the lake more accessible to all, meaning that there's now a paved path all the way.

The stream turns to the left, past the first of the major engineering efforts to make a paved path passable for wheels. There have been many tons of rock poured in here to build up an even roadbed wide enough to take a car or truck.

There are many opportunities to take one of the little trails down to the left beside the creek. Some day the powers that be will admit that, with the best of intentions on both sides, people and bikes on the same path don't mix. It's much more gratifying to the senses to walk along a bumpy, narrow footpath than a hard, straight road any time of the year.

At the Lawrence Avenue Bridge the paved path splits. Take a third, unpaved trail alongside the creek. Just past the bridge, there's a large sewer pipe crossing the valley on concrete pillars, well out of the reach of boys, flash floods, and other natural disasters.

This is the old original path, and you can tell by its depth that it was here long before the land was made safe for wheels.

A word about mosquitoes, especially in June and July. The usual explanation that only female mosquitoes bite, and then only because these poor mothers have to supply protein for the growth and health of their young, and that they'd just as soon have it from birds as from people, is interesting, but doesn't seem relevant. There's a lot of wetland around here (look to the right), and there are a lot, really a lot, of mosquito mommies out for your blood. Slather on the anti-mosquito goop, or be prepared to run like the wind. Even the most unathletic have been known to make a fair bid for the four-minute mile coming out of here. Be warned, be prepared, and then be cool.

There's another stretch where tons of rock have been used to create a bicycle path. To the right there's a high ridge of land approaching the creek at right angles. If you look back along the north face a short way, you'll see a path. That used to be the only way to get further down the creek.

If you do go up the hogsback, there's a path leading along its top and back down the right-hand side into a flatland. A little further on it becomes a wetland, complete with cattails and some open water. If you keep to the lower reaches of the bank, you can get around closer to the open water with dry feet. If you're into wetland watching, this is a great place to do it.

When the path splits, keep to the edge of the creek. When you come to a small creek burbling in from the right, follow it upstream to the footbridge.

A chain-link fence marks the edge of the Highland Creek Sewage Treatment Plant. Some days, with the wind in the right direction . . . .

Starting from the south side of the bridge, turn left, and head back down to the creek and follow it. The main path follows a dry stream-bed more or less straight ahead. When the river turns left, take the little path that strikes off to follow it. Continue on down beside the creek, and cross a stream coming from beneath the sewage treatment plant. Don't flinch: it drains water off the tops of the buildings, not from beneath them. The path climbs up somewhat towards the fence, then back down by the water. Keep an eye open in the muddy spots for prints—could be fox, coyote, white-tailed deer, raccoon or occasionally skunk; there's a lot of traffic along this trail.

Eventually you'll run out of trail. Turn to the right, and soon you're on the dry stream-bed trail. Follow this left to the main path.

There's a recent engineering solution to the problem of getting to the lake beyond the GO line—a long steel bridge. It will carry you right across beneath the rail bridge and around the corner, and may seem a little more solution than the problem requires. There used to be a pleasant trail up beside the stream, with no need to cross the tracks at all. But there's a long-term objective: eventually it's planned to have a section of the Trans-Canada Trail all along the lakeshore, and this can be part of that system.

Turning right off the bridge, it's possible to walk down to the beach, but stay up here and follow along beside the fence parallel to the GO line, until you come eventually to Beechgrove Drive below the sewage treatment conglomeration. Turn right up the road towards the parking lot, and then left into it. Walk across to the middle of the south side, to a gravel-surfaced path leading back towards the lake.

Continue along the trail, past the pond.

The path dips down and then rises to meet a row of posts joined by two strands of heavy cable. This will mark your route from here over to the filtration plant. The path is clear and easily followed.

There is a small trail out along the edge of the Scarborough Bluffs—often it is right at the very edge of the bluffs. In many places, anyone taking a misstep can slide over the edge. To do so means at least severe injury and perhaps death. Once a year, on average, someone decides to mess with these bluffs, necessitating search-and-rescue efforts, possibly a helicopter ride to the hospital, and thirty seconds of fame on the evening news. The trail described here will follow along the posted path.

Those buildings off to the left across the bay are the Pickering Nuclear Power Station.

With its wealth of open grassland, this is a great place to look for both bugs and birds; just don't go over the edge in pursuit of your monarch. While walking along this trail, don't be surprised to see a hawk or seagull gliding along on the updrafts just a short distance away.

Further on, the trail passes close to the East Point Sports Complex with, amongst other attractions, a washroom, often open during the warmer months. It's close enough to justify a detour if required. Walk right over to the fence, then right again along it to the gate. Head along the path to the central buildings. To rejoin the walk, just reverse course.

The Easterly Filtration Plant is set in the midst of a huge, open manicured meadow. Beyond that is a high chain-link fence marking the beginning of industrial land to the west. Keep to the posts for a little way, but then move over towards the bottom of the hills rising up towards the buildings. Continue on to the parking lot, heading towards the western end. Walk out to the crossroad and turn left.

On the other side of the road are the GO tracks with a ditch along beside them, bordered by tall phragmites. This road is short, and soon turns up to the right. Go straight along what appears to be an old road allowance running parallel to the tracks.

The chain-link fence makes a right-angled turn to the left, and the trail follows around it for a little way. To the right and below is a gorgeous little wooded wetland. There are lots of birds and willows, and it's just a delightfully swampy little spot to come and watch and listen on a warm, lazy summer afternoon.

At the park, continue around the swampy bit to the right, to a path angling a bit through the trees. Follow it towards some backyard fences, turning to the right again just before you reach them. Turn to the left when the fence ends, and keep a sharp eye out for an old fallen tree, as the trail angles off to the right again around it. Follow this wide trail along beside the tracks out to Morningside Road. Turn right, and about a block up there are bus stops on each side of the road.

GETTING BACK: For those using public transport, cross the road and take the southbound 116 Morningside bus back to Kennedy Subway Station. For those who left their car back at the parking lot, catch a 116 Morningside bus up to Kingston Road, then transfer to an 86A Scarborough bus back to the road leading to the parking lot.

WEST & SOUTHWEST HIGHLAND CREEK

DISTANCE: 7.5 kilometres

NOTE: While occasionally following paved paths, the trail is mostly through riverine lands and is not especially difficult for the first part. Near Lawrence there is a little difficulty along the edge of a bank. Along the north side of the Southwest Highland Creek tributary there are some short, steep hills, but it's mostly easy walking on well-defined trails after that.

GETTING THERE BY PUBLIC TRANSPORT: Take the Bloor/Danforth Subway to the LRT, the LRT to Ellesmere Station, and the 95 eastbound bus past Midland to the entrance to Birkdale Park.

GETTING THERE BY AUTOMOBILE: Drive to Ellesmere and Kennedy and park in the TTC lot. Either take the 95 eastbound bus a few blocks, or walk east to the creek, it's not really very far.

SUMMARY: This walk follows down the creek, mostly on trails across from the paved cycle paths, to Thompson Park, and down through the park on both paved paths and trails beside the creek to where the Southwest Highland Creek joins it. It then continues out along the north side of this creek for a ways, back through a woodland, then on down to where it meets West Highland Creek again, ending at Markham Road.

THE WALK: The sign reads Birkdale Ravine, and the paved path on the east side of the West Highland Creek leads down into a valley, the beginning of the walk.

Follow the paved path to a footbridge, and cross on it, passing a big old weeping willow at the corner. There's a road angling up the hill, but the walk follows a trail sharply to the left, down beside the creek.

At the next bridge, continue straight ahead. In a few moments begin edging over to the right, to pass around a small ravine where it begins at a storm sewer outlet. Once past, swing left with the old riverbank and the creek.

Up ahead there's a double or triple row of gabion baskets lining the creek edge, with one row set back from another, providing a ledge for you to walk on. At the far end it becomes narrow, but there's lots of growth to hold on to. Once past this stretch the trail moves away from the bank, and there's a steep climb up around another outlet and then down the other side. Go right down to the water, then there's another bank to scramble up, about a metre or so.

After this the trail follows right beside the creek edge. Watch for those places where erosion may have stolen some path, or undercut the ground beneath it.

The next long row of gabion baskets again have tops that form the path. At the end, there's a sort of trough behind the baskets, passable in dry weather. If it's wet, then you may have a bit of a scramble to get past here. This is as bad as the going gets, however, and it's soon past.

When the trail forks, stay left.

At the next large field, there's the usual path coming down from the right to cross over a bridge. The trail passes by a big set of blocks, heads around the fenced outlet, and down a trail to the left.

At Brimley Road, climb the bank beside the bridge and carefully cross.

Incidentally, as mentioned in the introduction to this watershed, it's just on the north side of this river, quite close by, that the remains of a First Peoples' village were discovered, dating back to about the year 1250. The whole site, including a burial ground, covered about 4 hectares.

On the other side there's a sign marked Thompson Memorial Park – Museum. There is a path down the other (far) side.

Keep the creek on your right and eventually, after walking through open parkland and back into the woods, you'll see a high bank ahead, directly across the path. When the creek dives into a big concrete double tunnel, go to the left and up a long flight of steps to the top.

Down the other side is a long wintertime toboggan run. At the bottom the creek emerges from its underground sojourn.

Stay on the east side of the creek, cross a bridge and walk on through a space filled with mature trees of many species. When the creek makes a sharp left, you'll come to a footbridge that carries a paved pathway straight across to the left, and through a hydro transmission corridor out to McGowan Road. Cross the bridge to the right and take a more challenging and interesting route.

At the bottom of the hill leading up to the hydro corridor, turn left along a rather dim path through the cedars. There's a flat space running along here, midway between the river and the corridor up to the right. It's treed with spruce and pine and the usual deciduous stuff, and is easiest walking close to the bottom of the bank—the trees are older here and there's more space.

The trail is easily followed but it can be slippery at times. It gets easier as you go along, and in time you come to the place where the hill stops, and it's all flat ahead. Follow along beside the creek to where it makes a right-angled turn to the right.

There's a parking lot up on top of another hill, and eventually you'll have to get up there. As you progress, the hill closes in and the walking becomes rougher.

When it gets too rough, stop for a breather, then climb to the top and proceed through the parking lot down to McCowan Road. Cross McCowan carefully—the traffic is usually heavy.

On the other side, walk left across the bridge and turn right down the paved path and follow it to the bridge at Lawrence Avenue. Walk under the bridge and turn sharply left. Soon you'll come to a bridge carrying a path up the hill to the right. Cross the bridge and go along the stream to the left.

There's a good bit of up-and-down along here. The creek is still small, trees have fallen across it in many places, and there's a close, intimate sense about the whole space.

There's a stream coming in from the right that's just about as big as West Highland Creek itself. This is the Southwest Highland Creek. The trail will follow it up a ways and then back on the other side.

You might note the tree stumps close to where the streams meet. A few years ago, one or two ambitious beaver were seriously considering a building site close by. Whether natural circumstances or the parks department changed their minds, they're long gone, leaving only this stumpy record. There's more recent beaver work further downstream.

The trail heads up the bank, and ahead is one of those square concrete storm-sewer access pipes. Coming down again to a flatland, you can see where mature trees have fallen over the creek because of erosion. In time you'll again begin to ascend the bank that has approached closely to the creek. You're soon just a short bit below someone's backyard.

The trail drops halfway down the bank and then goes up and down along a good path with only a few tricky bits. Finally the trail descends to creek level and crosses a footbridge.

On the other side, the most-travelled path proceeds up the hill to the right; however there's another, clearly visible, but less-worn trail curving up the hill towards the woods.

As the creek winds its way back towards the trail, there are concrete remains of what is probably an old mill dam. Streams of even this relatively small size were frequently dammed a century and a half ago. Remember that aside from muscle and horse or oxen, they were the only source of energy for sawing wood or grinding grain.

Follow that clear trail along until it meets West Highland Creek again.

Turn right along the stream, and you'll soon come to a footbridge with a small, concrete waterfall just upstream of it, causing a muted roar of white sound. Shortly you'll come to Bellamy Bridge.

If you wish to end your walk here walk up to the street, turn right to the bus stop, and catch the Number 9 bus north to the Scarborough Town Centre Station on the LRT. Most of the rest of this walk is through parkland, with one exception towards the end.

Past the bridge continue on through the park. Here and there are high metal poles, with two-storey birdhouses on top. These were probably intended to attract purple martins, but the house sparrows seem more interested.

After some more footbridges you'll come to a roofed picnic shed filled with expanded metal bench-seat combinations. At the next footbridge to the right cross, and immediately turn left. There's a well-used but unpaved path here, winding around through trees, first beside the stream, then back into the bushes. In time, it'll bring you out to Markham Road.

The Scarborough Golf and Country Club blocks any further progress along West Highland Creek, so climb up to the road.

GETTING BACK: Either walk north, or cross the street and take the 102 Markham bus north a bit to Lawrence Avenue. Cross and catch the 54 Lawrence East bus westbound to the Lawrence East LRT Station.

Another alternative is to walk back to the beginning along the paved path; it will be a shorter trip than the one coming down.

HIGHLAND WALK 5
CREEK HOPPER

DISTANCE: 7.5 kilometres
NOTE 1: You'll have to ford the creek six times, and depending on water level and weather, wet feet are a real possibility. Waterproof footgear or a willingness to wade are obligatory. Ice in winter can be dangerous.
NOTE 2: The shape and form of the creek are constantly changing. Certainly ice and high meltwaters have a powerful effect each spring. The exact location of the fords may change from year to year.
NOTE 3: There are a couple of places where you would be well advised to step carefully and hold on to something more solid than a companion.
GETTING THERE BY PUBLIC TRANSPORT: Take the Bloor Subway to Kennedy Station, then the LRT to Scarborough Town Centre. The 171 Progress East bus or the 134 will take you right to the creek at the corner of Markham Road and Progress Avenue. Just cross the bridge to the south side and turn left.

GETTING THERE BY AUTOMOBILE: The most likely parking spaces are in mall parking lots south of Progress Avenue. As with most of these walks, it may prove more convenient in the long run to park the car and take the bus.

SUMMARY: The walk travels from Markham Road south along Highland Creek. Because of steep banks it becomes necessary to cross the creek a number of times. The trail follows both sides of the creek south, first to Military Trail, then Morningside Park, and continues past the washrooms there and south beneath Morningside Bridge. It turns left, up through a unique woodland in the Scarborough campus of the University of Toronto, and finally rejoins a paved path down to Old Kingston Road.

THE WALK: Begin the walk down a gravelled road running east from Markham Road along the south side of Highland Creek. Closer to creek level the gravel surface ends, but there's still a wide, clear path to follow. When this path too ends, continue on a narrow footpath beginning half a metre up a bank and running to the right, into the woods.

Climb a bank about 1.5 metres high. There are a number of trails in here, but stay with the one nearest the creek.

At the first crossing the bank is steep on this side, but there's a stretch where large rocks have been poured into the creek to provide erosion protection. Climbing over these is the easiest path down to the water. A number of different groups of stepping stones ford the creek. This is the easiest crossing, so if it seems too difficult, you may want to choose some other walk.

In the field on the other side you may have to cast around until you pick up the trail again. It can become obscure in summer when the herbal growth gets exuberant.

The bank leading down to the next crossing looks steep, but getting down is not really difficult. Go to the left and you'll usually find enough stones sufficiently close together to make a dry crossing.

Again there's a field to cross, only to be met by the creek for a third time. Go to the left of the trail where there's a bar or small island close to the opposite bank. Look well to the left to find the stepping stones.

Once on the island look for a place where the stream narrows—there are some boulders to serve the purpose. The challenge comes at the other bank, because it's vertical. Pick your way along to the right to a climbable spot. Once on top, follow the creek to the trail.

Up ahead there's a short line of link fencing. To the left of that there's a wide gravel road curving down from Centennial College. It travels parallel to the creek and provides easy walking for a while, continuing in fits and starts right down to Ellesmere Road. The main thing it lacks to make it useful is bridges.

Down by the water at the next crossing there may be signs of animals. Most tracks have been made by hiking boots or dog paws, but there could also be raccoon, deer, coyote, duck or others.

Once again you'll have to look for rocks unless you're wearing rubber boots. There are usually lots of stones in the stream, and it's easy enough to add a couple more if necessary.

On the other side the gravel path continues to a big old pine. From there follow the trail until it leads to the stream again. Follow the gravel and boulder bar as far as possible, then climb the bank. You'll have to hunt inland for a trail. Duck beneath a couple of fallen logs, one with its end stuck up the bank, and the trail leads out to the creek beside a pair of hemlocks. There is usually a group of stepping stones in this area, but you'll have to cast about for them. The creek is very changeable in this area.

The path ends at a high clay bank directly ahead on the other side of the creek. A thin trail leads off to the left and down onto a sand bar. There are some rocks and stepping stones, but they tend to be widely spaced. You can either depend on waterproof boots, or take off shoes and socks and wade. Or live with wet feet.

The path leads up to Military Trail. Cross the bridge, turn right down the gravel path and follow it to the end. It stops, after spreading out a bit. Turn left and follow the trail along parallel to the creek, which has now turned sharply left.

Continue over towards a fallen tree, duck and continue. The trail passes through another large fallen tree, out of which someone has cut a piece to allow passage. The trail follows right beside the bank edge in many places, with no margin for error in placing a foot. The water down below is not deep enough to be threatening, but the sheer drop could do some serious harm to a human body. Step carefully, lean left and keep a hand on something solid.

When the creek and trail begin to diverge, start climbing gently upwards. Watch out, there are a couple of sheer drops. Up among some cedars the trail widens momentarily and, because it slopes towards the river, can be tricky when wet and slick with mud. Keep well left, within reach of some trees.

At the peak of the trail, right beside a large cedar, there's the edge of a hydro right-of-way, with the first power line up above. Take the left fork, directly uphill. It is the last hard climb. Continue onwards and upwards to the top, where the trail meets the edge of the flat, mown right-of-way. Turn right along the mown edge in a long curve, and at the wooden hydro pole, take the fainter trail leading over to a big metal pylon straight ahead.

At the foot of the pylon you'll have a good view out across the creek and beyond to the Ellesmere Bridge. In front is a clear trail. It leads downwards, way down. Follow the trail to Ellesmere Road.

For anyone wishing to end their walk here, there are a couple of buses running along Ellesmere Road. The 95 goes to the Ellesmere Station and the 133 to Scarborough Town Centre. Catch one on this, the north side, and it will return you to the Bloor Subway.

After the trail leaves the bridge it parts company with the creek and eases off to the left across a wide meadow. Beyond the sumac there's another wood, and just at the edge there's a long, gently sloping ramp leading upward through the bank. At the top the trail turns right through the pines. Follow over the hill, and descend to a fork, taking the right path beside the fluffy pine. Cross another meadow into more woods again. Go left to an ancient pine, then turn sharply right. Back at the creek, go straight. The other branch goes out into a point of land in the centre of a bow in the creek—a pleasant side-trip for anyone so inclined.

The trail winds around and eventually ends up at creek level on a sand and gravel bar. At the end there's a road coming down from Morningside Park. At the top the path curves around to the left and leads to a washroom.

Continue on from the washroom, away from the creek to a parking lot. Keep walking along the paved path up and over the small hill, and look for a light standard on the right. Just past it, leave the pavement and follow the trail running to the right down the valley.

After the wooded glen, there's an old orchard. The smell of cider vinegar in the late summer and early fall can be almost overpowering.

On the far side of the orchard there's another washroom on the right. Turn left along the bottom of the bank to yet another washroom, far across the green. This one is open all year round and could be a good place to take a break.

Past the washrooms and across the footbridge there's another bus opportunity. Across the parking lot you can follow the path out to Morningside Avenue, where the Morningside bus will take you to Kennedy Subway Station.

To continue with the walk, turn right through the parking lot and on to meet the paved pathway. Turn left towards the Morningside Bridge. Just past the bridge there's a sign welcoming all to the Scarborough campus of the University of Toronto. Past the sign the trail leads off to the left, away from the paved path.

There's a small stream trickling through its own little gully, at right angles to the path, and the main trail turns left. The objective is to get to the other side of this stream and pick up the trail as it continues ahead. At the fork, take the one to the left and climb to a higher level. This is not a well-used trail, and you may have to push things aside in places to get through.

At the next fork stay right, and watch the trail slowly disappearing. Look for a group of three pines (or one pine split into three almost at ground level). From here you can see a large fallen tree ahead and a little to the left. Duck (or crawl) under it and you'll rediscover the trail. It's really tight down here, but there is an open space up the middle.

The soil here is very thin; in fact, there's hardly any at all, yet we're walking through a forest. Now look down and see the vast network of roots on top of the ground. The trees are mostly hemlock, and they seem able to survive, even flourish, in this environment. Certainly there's not a great deal of competition from other species. Watch your step and watch the trail.

This whole area is filled with woodland flowers in spring, and you can spend a most enjoyable hour or two searching them out among the roots.

Meeting another, clearer trail, go left. A patch of green grass leads up a hill, and at the top are university buildings. Instead of going up towards the buildings, turn right along a wide path. A little further on it becomes paved and leads to the path at a footbridge leading across the creek to other parts of the campus.

You're entering bike country again. Be careful.

No more brush-bashing, creek crossing or mountain climbing. Just relax and enjoy the scenery from here on. Listening for bird calls or bicycle bells, follow the path around and across a footbridge.

Just before Old Kingston Road, off the path to the left there's a bronze plaque commemorating the early settlers and their mills. It's worth a look. It's easy to forget that what we may take as an afternoon's pastime was almost the whole world to some a century and a half ago. Remember that the town of York, today's downtown Toronto, was the better part of a day's travel distant, and there weren't a lot of neighbours close at hand.

Just before going up to the road, the path forks. Take the left fork beneath the bridge, and follow it around and up to road level.

On the other side of the bridge there's a path leading back down towards the creek. Anyone who's still full of vim and vigor and feels up to another 7 kilometres can proceed down this pathway and, where it meets another coming down from the left, begin Highland Walk 3. If that's not appealing, continue on up the hill.

GETTING BACK: Walk up to the traffic lights, turn right and continue to the bus stop at Kingston Road. Get on the 86 bus to Kennedy Station on the Bloor Subway line. If the car is back near the beginning of the walk, from Kennedy take either the 171 or 134 bus back to Markham Road and Progress Avenue.

ELLESMERE RAVINE STREAM

DISTANCE: 3.5 kilometres

NOTE: This is a relatively short walk, intended more for making frequent stops and looking than for setting speed records. Much of it follows no clear trail, there are a couple of long climbs and descents, and the stream must be crossed a number of times on stepping stones or logs. Drowning is not likely, but a wet foot is possible. Having said this, it remains that this walk has a unique, jewel-like quality about it, and is well worth the effort.

GETTING THERE BY PUBLIC TRANSIT: Take the Bloor/Danforth Subway east to Kennedy Station, and get on the 116 Morningside bus. Ride the bus to the bottom of the hill where Morningside crosses Highland Creek, at the main entrance to the park. Cross the road to the park entrance.

GETTING THERE BY AUTOMOBILE: Drive north on Morningside Avenue from Lawrence Avenue or south from Ellesmere Road to the entrance, signed Morningside Park, Highland Creek, just north of the creek on the west side of the road. Park in the parking lot, then walk back to the park entrance.

SUMMARY: The walk travels from the park entrance, following a path skirting the old beaver pond to an inner parking lot, north to the Ellesmere Ravine Stream, across Ellesmere Road and north beside the stream, through a hydro right-of-way to Keeler Boulevard and west to Neilson.

THE WALK: In early spring, the hillside near the park entrance is a great place to find both white and the rarer red trilliums. There is a trail up the hill a bit, winding down to the bottom later on. To the right is one of the few homes of skunk cabbages in Toronto.

Curve around to the left following the hill base. Walk up the hill just a bit to a trail coming down from the ridge, and turn right to follow it. It will lead left, through some cedar trees, to a road. Turn right and follow that to a parking lot.

On the other side of the road to the right, cross the little field, and go through a row of brown posts. Beyond them, climb a little hill, and follow the path to the right. At the fork, follow the right-most trail across a small meadow and over back towards the wetland again.

Walk on through thick herbaceous growth, and past old storm-blasted willows. Soon the trail swings to the left and begins to ascend a long, gradual path leading towards the top of a high ridge.

Partway up there's an intersecting trail: turn right along it across the side of the hill. This trail may become somewhat faint in places, so the guiding principle is, if in doubt, stay fairly close to the bottom of the hill and the flat wetland to the right.

Up ahead, Ellesmere Road is visible and audible. Down below is the Ellesmere Stream.

You'll have to climb the steep bank to cross the road, and that may be a little easier from the other side of the stream. Crossing the stream is simple enough, except in flood time. The stream takes the easy way through a huge culvert.

Once up on the road, cross and go down the bank on the left (west) side, back to the stream.

A trail runs along the edge of the bank, but there's also a path a bit to the left, safer in wet weather. This trail is often narrow and can be slippery, so walk carefully.

There are some huge granite boulders in the stream bed, inherited from the last ice age melt nine or ten thousand years ago. Geologically speaking, nothing much else has happened around here lately, except for the trickle creating this ravine.

Where there are some gabion baskets and a little dam there's a well-used path crossing the ravine left to right. Take this opportunity to cross to the other side.

From here on, trails become ever more a matter of opinion. The objective is to get up this stream dry shod, and with a minimum of climbing. There are a couple of climbs definitely required, and these will be described. For the rest, cross and recross as desired.

In the summer there are a wide variety of wildflowers down in the little meadows beside the stream. And fungi seem to be everywhere. There are all the usual mushrooms, but here there may also be a bright red slime as big as a fist, there, a weird ivory-coloured blob sprouting from the side of a dead tree. You're in a deep little valley, hidden from the rest of the world, almost in silence. This is one of those rare places seeming to have a touch of magic about them, a place where something special can happen. This stream embodies quiet stillness.

You're coming to the most challenging spot on this walk. Up ahead is the remains of a steel weir across the stream, once about 3 metres high. Now the steel pilings have fallen down, and erosion has caused several trees to fall across the stream just below it. The best way is to go back downstream a little until you find a granite boulder almost as big as a small car. Just beyond this is the bottom of a trail leading up the east bank to the very top. Once you've climbed it, you'll see another trail going back down. Follow it back to the stream.

Soon the ravine narrows, there's another steel pile weir up ahead, and there are an increasing number of trees lying across the stream, making it virtually impassable. It's time to begin a long ascent up the left bank. Looking up, you'll see a line of hydro wires passing overhead. You need to come up at the near edge of the hydro right-of-way. Any path is a good path.

Up at the top, you may have to brush-bash a little to get to the cleared space. Once there, you'll see houses up ahead along the left side of the right-of-way. Just before reaching them, turn right on a path coming from the left, and follow it down a steep-sided gully across the right-of-way.

This path is old and deeply worn, and can be muddy and slippery at times. The stream is now visible again, down to the right. Partway across, another gully cuts through the trail.

The trail continues up a hillside, towards where a culvert dumps the stream down a long concrete chute into its valley. What appears to have been the original stream valley goes off up to the left. It's a steep little climb.

At the top, proceed across Military Trail to a park on the other side, and turn sharply left to enter the old stream bed. Why the stream was entombed in concrete and the stream bed was left open is a mystery. After crossing beneath a footbridge, the stream bed just peters out. Continue across the park.

At Keeler Boulevard turn left, down through suburban streets to the traffic lights at Neilson. Cross Neilson, and cross again to the right and go up to the bus shelter.

GETTING BACK: For those travelling by public transport, take the 133 southbound bus to Scarborough Centre Station on the LRT.

Those who left their car at Morningside can also take the 133, but transfer to the 85 bus east to Morningside, where you again transfer to the southbound 116 bus down to the Morningside Park entrance.

MAKING TRACKS

The flowers are gone, the birds are gone, the bugs are gone, the leaves are gone. What's left to be seen in the woods in midwinter? The answer is, lots!

In February there's often snow on the ground, and when things walk or move in the snow they leave tracks. Look for the dainty little holes left by a hunting fox. You'll know you have the right ones if they zig, then zag, then stop, and there's a sploosh. Our red-haired friend coursed back and forth, searching, until his or her keen ears picked up the minutest scratching sound from beneath the snow. There was a jump straight up in the air, a flurry of snow, a snap, and the world had one less mouse or vole, and a fox that would live a little longer.

Deer are fun. They will lead you where no one has ever gone before: be prepared to duck and climb. And unless there's a wild goat roaming around, they're the only animal you're likely to meet in or near the woods with a split hoof at the end of each leg. You can tell where they've browsed because they rip off twigs and leaves, rather than cutting them cleanly. Their scats look a little like giant raisins that haven't shrunk and become all wrinkled. If you're lucky, you'll find a bed; a dent in the snow made by the deer's body as it rested. Often it will be in or beside a grove of white cedar, protection from the freezing wind.

Around open water, Canada goose prints are clear—big, webbed, birdie feet. If the tracks are about twice as big as a goose, long and narrow but with the same characteristic webbing between the toes, chances are there's a beaver in the neighbourhood. Their forepaws are more hand-shaped, like a raccoon's. And as for raccoons, you're liable to find their tracks anywhere from the local creek to your garbage can. They rest during the winter, but they don't hibernate.

The other animal that's becoming increasingly common all over the northeast is the coyote. Coyote tracks are quite recognizable, once you get used to looking for them. They're about the same size as those of a medium-sized dog, but more diamond shaped, with the nails of the middle two toes close together. A dog's track is messy, as the paw is fairly broad and each toe has nails. A coyote's trail is neat. They don't bound about and play, but they don't get fed at home either. If they're moving, they're hunting.

To get a feel for the thing, imagine yourself in a cedar copse on a crisp February day. The first thing you notice are the still-intact bones of a hind leg sticking up from a mound of fur. Most of the back end of the animal has been devoured, leaving head, pelt, tail and mostly intact skeleton. It's the remains of a young raccoon, not yet fully grown.

Perhaps you were here to capture the lonely, frigid image of a stream babbling through a winter wood. Streams do babble; they tinkle too, and this one does both as it tumbles beneath the snow-covered fallen trees that criss-cross a miniature ravine.

You may never know what caught your eye, why you shifted your attention away from water to bone, but there it is. Who dunnit? A tale of mortal drama lies written in the new snow. Tracing back along the tracks, perhaps you'll be able to reconstruct what happened.

A young raccoon had been patrolling the open waters of the stream, looking for crayfish or anything else edible, when along came a coyote. The coyote stopped. The raccoon flinched back in fear. If there had been any sizeable body of open water around the raccoon would have been safe, because he could outswim the coyote any day. But there was only the stream.

For a single coyote to kill a raccoon is no easy task. The coyote circled around and darted in, but fang met only fang. It was a draw until a second coyote joined in. While number one kept the front end busy, number two attacked from the rear. It was finished quickly.

Division of spoils gained through violence is never easy for us mammals. Both coyotes claimed the victor's share. One dragged the carcass a short distance away, attempting to take ownership. That didn't work, so he, or she, dragged it again.

Finally, probably after much growling and snapping, most of the choice bits were eaten and the pair trotted off together to find a secluded spot in which to lay down and let digestion take over.

The fact that predators survive proves that this sort of incident must occur frequently. There are rarely human observers, as they would upset the balance of predator and prey. You might see the brush marks of an owl's wing on the snow, ending the progression of mouse tracks between clumps of grass. In summer you'll come across a pile of feathers, or part of a skeleton. Sometimes, if you watch the ground closely, you may well find the unmarked body of a jumping mouse or mole, dead simply of old age. Very often this will be your only opportunity to view these tiny creatures closely.

When you see tracks, stop. What happened? Who was doing what? Who lived? Who died? Snow and mud preserve records for a little while, and learning to read those records requires observation, but more importantly, empathy. They have the power to bring you closer to that real world of which we are all a part.

CHAPTER 6

THE ROUGE RIVER
WATERSHED

Rouge Park is the largest natural and cultural heritage park in an urban area in North America, encompassing 4,700 hectares of valley and tablelands stretching from Lake Ontario to the Oak Ridges Moraine. It extends well beyond the city, and even the part that's in the city is no ordinary city park. So far there are no paved bicycle paths and no great expanses of alien grasses, all neatly trimmed. Partly this is because the Rouge is a park in the making, but more important, it's because the whole idea is to keep wild what is wild, and to preserve ecosystems that have evolved over the last century.

Although the Province of Ontario created it, Rouge Park is not exactly a provincial park either. It's set up to operate under the direction of a board of directors drawn from all levels of government, plus interest groups.

The purpose of designating this watershed as parkland is to protect it. Since the beginning of the nineteenth century the pressure has been on to do something "useful" with the land. First there was logging, but it was pretty well logged out by the mid-1800s. The high sand ridge running down between the two rivers to their confluence was called the "Mast Road," because great pine logs were hauled down it and dumped into the combined rivers, and then floated down to Lake Ontario. There they were hoisted onto ships and sent on their way across the ocean, to become masts for the British Navy. Some were 150 or more years old and a metre or more in diameter. When the big ones had all been cut down, the lesser trees were squared off, carried, dumped and floated downstream also. And not only the white pine trees but also maples, beech, oak, ash, and anything that looked as if it could be cut into planks was either sawn up locally or shipped overseas. The oldest trees we have today, especially between Twyn Rivers Road and Finch, date back a century and a half to the time when lumbering ended.

Of course this process produced a lot of treeless land. On the plains surrounding the ravines the soil made good farmland, but down the four levels of the ravines the land became progressively less useful for growing a paying crop because of all the sand and gravel. Never mind; the sand and gravel had a value too—for road building and rooftops.

The beach of old Lake Iroquois runs through part of the Metro Toronto Zoo and is visible at the Beare Road Landfill, just up the road from where a couple of the walks begin or end, at Pearse House. The whole valley has huge deposits of sand and gravel from ice ages past, and these were exploited intensively. You can see the results most obviously just south of Beare Road Landfill. Further south from that, the land cover is loam and clay, so it was left alone.

But it wasn't just the flat tablelands that were gouged out and hauled off. Between 1956 and 1960, over 40 hectares of bottomland, right down to the very riverbeds themselves, were scraped clear of gravel. This happened along 3 kilometres of the Rouge River south of Finch Avenue and west of Sewells Road, in part, where Cedarbrae and Brookside Golf Clubs are today. There were also scrapings taken along about 3.5 kilometres of the Little Rouge, from Twyn Rivers Drive north to Plug Hat Road. Gouge marks, spoil mounds and pits still remain from those riverside operations.

And when the trees have all been cut and the gravel trucked away, what do we do with what's left? Why, we make it into a garbage dump. Then we spread some earth over top and call it a landfill site, in this case the Beare Road Landfill.

There was one other indignity inflicted on the stream, which in fact didn't work out all that badly. Down in the wetlands, where the river flowed into Lake Ontario, someone had an idea for a unique housing development. Dig canals through the marsh (which was done), build houses (which was not done), and call it the Venice of the North. Fortunately the Great Depression came along and brought an end to the whole depressing idea. What's left is the best remaining example of lakeshore marsh in Toronto.

It was during and after the time that earthmovers were raping the streams of the Rouge that a growing number of people began to see that perhaps destroying Toronto's last natural river system for the sake of building yet more ticky-tacky might not be the greatest idea of the century. There were many factors leading to this rising tide of opinion, including a burgeoning awareness of what our ever-increasing population was doing to the whole world. Nevertheless it still took close to thirty years to persuade the provincial government to declare the whole watershed a provincial park.

The pressures to make exceptions, to "open up" the watershed, to "make it pay its way" will not disappear.

One last word about the park aspect of the watershed. There is still privately owned land within the boundaries, including the Metro Toronto Zoo, a golf course, and some farms and homes. Just exactly where you're welcome to walk is still unclear, although the zoo is out of bounds for obvious reasons. One thing is certain—if walkers show respect for the rights and needs of others, everyone will be the happier. If you do go off-trail, be sure you know where you are. Private land is private. Zoo land is private and possibly dangerous. The railway lines are active, the trains move fast, tracks and bridges are used frequently, and "Trespassers Will be Prosecuted."

As with the other watersheds, this one has a history.

Like the Humber, the Rouge was also a route to the north and Lake Huron— gateway to the furs of the other great lakes and all the lakes and rivers of the Canadian Shield. It also had the appeal of occupying a neutral stretch between the native tribes to the east and west. Neither river was navigable after the first 2 kilometres or two, so the choice was six of one, a half dozen of the other.

Shortly after the Iroquois took over, they established a village on a rise just east of the mouth of the Rouge. They called it Ganetsekwyagon. In 1669–70, two priests of the Sulpician order came from Quebec to convert the locals. They were well received, and the next year the order established a permanent mission.

As settlement proceeded, first there was lumber and then grain to ship; it certainly couldn't go by road. In addition to the market in York, there were hungry people in the United States, accessible through Oswego at the other end of the lake. Some enterprising individuals built docks, and even established boatyards at both the Rouge and Highland Creeks, where a number of wooden ships were built. Some of the most notable included Captain Hadley's schooner *Duke of York*, built in the early 1800s. She was reputed to have been the fastest sailor on the lake. In 1825–26 a steam-powered vessel named the *Canada* was built. The last schooner was built and launched there in 1843.

If you ever have the feeling that you've now seen just about everything there is to see in the Rouge, consider these findings, established when the Ontario Ministry of Natural Resources did an ecological survey of the valley in 1991:

- one quarter of all of Ontario's flora are found here
- there are 762 plant species—5 nationally rare, 1 provincially rare and 92 regionally rare
- 55 species of fish swim in the upper and lower sections
- 225 species of birds fly through each year, and 123 species breed here
- 27 species of mammals wander the woods and meadows
- 19 species of reptiles and amphibians hide in grass and stream

Gee, they missed the insects. There are probably a few of those too.

Granted, the survey and numbers pertain to the whole watershed, from Oak Ridges Moraine down to the lake, but you can be sure that most species are represented in the section south of Steeles Avenue.

The watershed of the Rouge is the wildest of the five watersheds underlying Toronto. For all that it has been abused, it is the least touched by human hands. During the week especially, but also in off seasons and on the weekends, it's possible to walk some of these trails for hours and see at the most one or two other people. But there are some stretches, mostly south of Pearse House at the Zoo Road, which have been more heavily used and need some recovery time. Most of the trails described here follow footpaths established through occasional use. The official park trails, which in most cases are easier walking, lead through those lands having received the more extensive use. In some places there are horse trails cut 30 centimetres deep into the sand over many years. And although forbidden, riders of trail bikes, which also gouge out these sand-based paths very quickly, also use these trails all too often. Even in this large area, there is evidence of too many people spreading out and creating mud flats where plants and young trees should be growing.

As described in earlier chapters, some intensely used parks in the city are being fenced off in places, to protect both flora and fauna from dogs, children and trail bikes. It's sad. It's sad that kids can't run over the hills and yell and slide down the banks. It's sad that dogs can't chase squirrels through the underbrush and splash through the mud and streams. It is sad, but it's also necessary when there are just to many people using too little territory. It would be even sadder if portions of the Rouge Watershed had to suffer the same fate as the others.

Look again at the number of rare species of plants located in 1991. If you pick one of them to take for the vase on the dining room table, to be shrivelled and dead the next day, you could be very much like the person who raised a stick to beat the last carrier pigeon to death. In order to protect the continued existence of this ecosystem, especially south of Pearse House, please be considerate—don't pick the flowers and do stick to the trails.

ROUGE WALK 1
THE WILD EAST SIDE

DISTANCE TO STEELES AVENUE: 6 kilometres. If the distance to the 53B bus stop is included, add 5 kilometres, for a total of 11 kilometres.
NOTE 1: This is a point-to-point walk with a possible turn-around at Meadowvale Road. The nearest public transit stop on Steeles Avenue is about 5 kilometres to the west after the walk's end, and the 53B bus runs only during the day, Mon-

day to Friday. You may want to loop this trail with Rouge Walk 2, adding an additional 6 kilometres, for a total of 12 kilometres.

NOTE 2: There are wet patches and high, steep hills. The trail disappears frequently, and although there is little actual brush-bashing, you may have to lean your way through the vegetation in places. Waterproof footwear is recommended in spring, or following wet weather.

GETTING THERE BY PUBLIC TRANSIT: The 85 Sheppard bus runs directly to the zoo from the Yonge, and it's also possible to take the 86A bus from Kennedy Subway Station to Meadowvale Road, or sometimes to the zoo. In either case, leave the bus just before it turns left across the bridge to the zoo. There is a designated bus stop there.

GETTING THERE BY AUTOMOBILE: Drive to Meadowvale Road and take the zoo turnoff. At the bridge leading to the zoo, turn right. The road deadends, and there is parking space available beside the road way.

SUMMARY: The walk crosses the Little Rouge River and proceeds north along the east side, following existing trails wherever possible, to the bridge at Meadowvale Road. After a brief walk along Meadowvale, the trail again swings off to parallel the river. Crossings are made beneath two railroad bridges and one wide hydro right-of-way. There is a brief passage close to an operating farm, and the walk ends at Steeles Avenue. It is possible to return following the Rouge Valley 2 walk along the west side of the river.

THE WALK: Getting off the bus or leaving the car, walk down the road ahead towards the gate. To the right is a fine old house from another era, obviously lovingly restored; it's home of the Pearse House Rouge Valley Conservation Centre.

Access to the walk is around the left end of the gate and down the road, towards the Little Rouge River at the bottom.

Up on top of the hill opposite is the Bear Road Sanitary Landfill site. At the bottom of the hill is an electricity generation plant powered by gas from old garbage. Just this side of the generating plant, there's a railway line that you'll be reminded of fairly often—it's a busy line.

Down at the bottom of the hill, take the trail that goes down to the other side of the river on the left. There's often a trail through the scrub growth beside the river, but don't count on it.

Like all of Toronto's rivers and streams, the water might not be much more than a trickle or it could be a roaring torrent, depending on time of year and recent weather. If it's high and fast, do not underestimate its power and danger, not only to children and pets, but to momentarily careless adults as well.

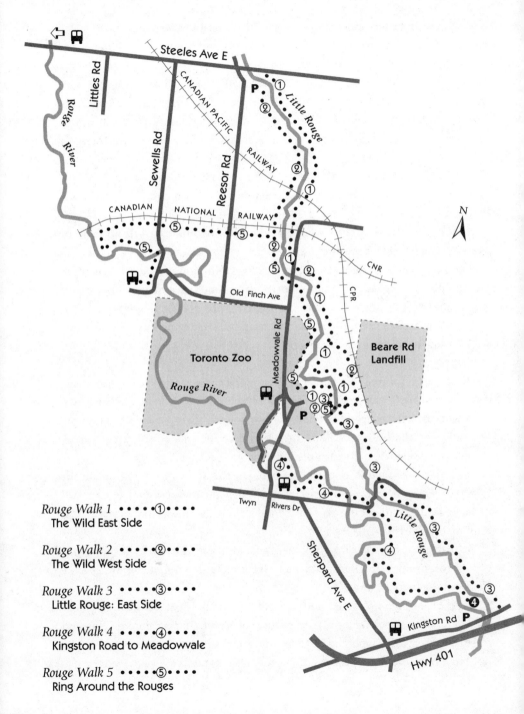

Steeles Ave E
Littles Rd
Rouge River
Sewells Rd
CANADIAN PACIFIC
Reesor Rd
RAILWAY
Little Rouge
P
CANADIAN NATIONAL RAILWAY
Old Finch Ave
Meadowvale Rd
N
CNR
CPR
Toronto Zoo
Rouge River
Beare Rd Landfill
P
Twyn Rivers Dr
Sheppard Ave E
Little Rouge
Kingston Rd
P
Hwy 401

Rouge Walk 1 • • • • ①• • • •
The Wild East Side

Rouge Walk 2 • • • • ②• • • •
The Wild West Side

Rouge Walk 3 • • • • ③• • • •
Little Rouge: East Side

Rouge Walk 4 • • • • ④• • • •
Kingston Road to Meadowvale

Rouge Walk 5 • • • • ⑤• • • •
Ring Around the Rouges

In the wood, spring flowers abound, including trilliums, bloodroot and even jack-in-the-pulpits. Before the trees' leaves pop out, it's possible to spend the whole day with a camera in just this little woodland alone. This season comes unannounced and passes quickly; you'll have to watch closely.

The trail goes over beside the riverbank, where you meet a well-worn path leading up to the fields above. For now, keep to the river.

Follow the groove down to the next lower level. Next take a ramp that slopes gently up to the right. Continue until the way becomes impassable, then scramble up that little hill to the right, using the roots and trees provided to help.

At the top of the hill, again there's no particular trail, but as you move away from the river, you'll come to an old, overgrown road. Follow it past a stack of old discarded culverts, and passing them on the left, continue on down to a flat, where there's a kind of trail.

All through this walk you'll come across trails. They could be people trails or deer trails or both—neither species holds a prejudice against using the results of the other's efforts. Keep an eye open for scats, hoofprints and occasional rubs where a buck has rubbed its antlers against some sapling, removing both bark and the velvety antler covering in the process. If the trail goes through an obstruction too low, too tangled or too small for you, you're probably on a deer trail.

A barn atop the opposite bank marks a sharp right turn. The building is part of the zoo establishment, so don't be surprised if you hear some odd sounds coming from it.

To the right there's a trail going up into a grove of cedar. Follow it out of the trees to a kind of groove running along the foot of the hill. To the left is the river, and you can also see where a trail once went along the edge of the hill. Erosion has made life difficult, and you'll have to take another path up this hill.

Turn to the right along the bottom of the hill until you come to a place where another path comes in from the right. To the left, the disturbed earth marks the place where, with time and care, you can climb to the top of this steep old bank. By the way, the purpose of following established paths and trails whenever possible is to save the hillside growth. It's fragile, and once gone, there's nothing much to hold the soil in place and, well, there goes the neighbourhood.

If you get tired, stop for a moment. Great discomfort is not a badge of honour— it's a mark of misjudgment.

At the top the trail splits; take the left fork along the edge of the bank. At the main trail take the lesser trail to the left, just this side of the stakes.

Over to the right there's a large dent in the land, once one of the quarries in the area, now part of a field that's hunting ground for coyotes and hawks. This

whole large area is being reformed to create more diverse habitat and educational exhibits. As you skirt the tree line along here, it suddenly turns out into the field directly across the path. Burrow into the left corner, and you'll find a ramp going down into the valley below. Once there, go straight ahead and a bit to the right, away from the trail and towards the top of the bank. Closer to the edge there's a trail coming up from below. Turn right along it. On the left there's a ravine carrying a stream into the river. It's quite deep and broad near the river end, quickly narrowing as the stream climbs over boulders, up towards the rail line to the right

There's no specific trail down into the ravine, but the hill is relatively gentle. Go upstream until you find a narrow point with a climbable bank on the other side. Once across, follow the stream down to the main river, then head upstream along the river.

When the river in one of its frequent meanders cuts directly across in front of you, follow it to the right. There's not much choice, really.

There are different levels here, and if you stop and look you can see how, over thousands of years, the river has meandered different places at different levels, leaving these flats at various elevations.

When the river wanders off to the left again, just continue along more or less straight ahead to a trail, faint but perceptible, up along the side of the hill. It stops climbing just below the field at the top, indicating that it's probably a deer trail. They don't like to be silhouetted against the open sky, preferring a background that makes the most of their camouflage colouring.

Soon you'll meet a much more heavily used trail, crossing from the tableland at the top and continuing back down the hill to your left.

This is a well-used path, and it used to be bare earth, slippery and downright dangerous in places. There was even a section that ran straight downhill, where a rope and ladder were provided. That's all changed now: there are steps and railings all the way down.

At the bottom, deep in the cedars, there's a clear trail beside the river until the main trail angles up again to the right. There begin to be more people, and dog and trail bike signs as the trail approaches Meadowvale Road.

Before this was officially designated a park, there was some maintenance and cleanup work done by people who enjoyed coming here and felt they would like to put something back in. Let's hope they consider it worthwhile to continue.

Where Meadowvale Road crosses the Little Rouge River is the only turn-around point in this walk. As mentioned at the beginning, there's no handy TTC at the end or along the route, so for anyone who's had enough, turn around and retrace the path. At the top of the steps, you might try the trail across the field. No trail looks the same from both directions, so be prepared for surprises.

Cross the road and walk along to the right for a ways, past a clutter of signs, to a path to the left with a chain across it between two posts. Step over, and away you go along the bank. From here to the first railway bridge, there are many remainders of tree farms.

You'll be crossing the bottom end of private property allotments along here, so it's important to keep on the path beside the bank—but not too close.

After crossing the bottom of a long backyard, there's a set of steps down to the left, making your descent considerably easier than some. In time you'll come to a large, stone fire circle, and just beyond it a low bank, with the remains of a water pump and enclosure at the top. At the next split in the trail, keep to the left.

When the trail is blocked by an abandoned railway embankment, one trail goes up over it, the other goes down to the left beside the river. If the river is especially high you'll have to go over the embankment. Usually there's just enough space to slowly and carefully edge along beside the water. A clump of sandbar willow in the way can be a challenge.

Just past the bridge there are a couple of trails, or perhaps "disturbed areas" would be a better term, leading up the bank to the right. You may have to push your way in through the shrubs to an old fence corner. Up along the fence a bit there's a trail running through it. Follow it to the left.

Where the path comes down from the right, turn along it to the right until you come to another trail going to the left, through regularly spaced evergreens. Keep tending to the left, back towards the river, and in time you'll get there.

On the other side of the next railroad bridge, go up the hill a bit to a place where the gully is narrow enough to cross comfortably. Out ahead is a very wide hydro right-of-way, with a farmed field beneath it, often planted with corn in the summer. The easiest path across the right-of-way is right at the edge of the field.

At the corner of the field there's a ridge coming in from the right. Walk to where the field meets the ridge, and go down to a roadway leading back up into a farm. If you continue over to the bank you'll find the hint of a trail along the edge. Shortly you'll come to the farm's backyard, running right up to the lip of the bank, which falls away sharply due to erosion. This is a good demonstration of what happens when the trees along a bank are removed: there's nothing to hold the soil in place, and things go downhill rapidly. There's a great view of the valley, though.

Proceed smartly across the lawn, and go to a trail diving down into the trees along the edge of the eroded cut. Take the descent parallel to the river leading to the plain below; don't follow the deer trail to the right.

Beside the river, walk along gravel banks, keeping clear of the willows. As you follow around a bow in the river the bank begins to rise, and there seems to be a hint of a path along here.

Above the river again, travel along the field edge to what looks like a wagon trail going down towards the river. Follow it down.

From here on there will be no more trails of any consequence, so just walk along parallel to the river, finding the least difficult passage. It's a nice flat wooded space all along here, with a good mixture of young and old trees. You'll encounter a meandering stream two or three times, and can follow an old stream bed towards the end. On the river there is what appears to be the remains of a dam— large concrete buttresses still standing. It may be what's left of one of the many mills built along the Rouge in earlier times.

The trail and Steeles Avenue seem to be on a slowly converging collision course, and eventually the two meet.

GETTING BACK: Those wishing to continue back on the other side of the Little Rouge River should cross the river and then consult Rouge Walk 2.

As noted at the beginning, there is a bus stop about 5 kilometres to the west along Steeles Avenue. The 53B bus runs Monday to Friday from 6:00 A.M. to about 6:30 P.M.

ROUGE WALK 2
THE WILD WEST SIDE

DISTANCE: 6 kilometres. Add 5 kilometres from the bus. This walk is most easily accessible when looped from Rouge Walk 1.

NOTE 1: Unless you have someone to drive you to the start, this walk can only be taken Monday to Friday because of limiting bus schedules.

NOTE 2: This is a fairly demanding, point-to-point walk. The only public transit approach is from bus 53B, 5 kilometres to the west, Monday to Friday. There are wet patches and one stream to cross. There are also some really steep climbs and descents. Trails are occasional.

GETTING THERE BY PUBLIC TRANSPORT: Monday to Friday, take the 129 bus from Scarborough Town Centre Subway Station north to Steeles Avenue, then transfer to the westbound 53 bus to the end of the line. Walk 5 kilometres to Reesor Road, where the walk begins.

GETTING THERE BY AUTOMOBILE: Note that, at the other end, if you don't have someone meeting you, the only way back by public transport is limited to weekdays; see above. Or you can loop with Rouge Walk 1.

Drive along Steeles Avenue to Reesor Road; turn right and then left into a parking lot.

SUMMARY: The walk begins from Steeles Avenue, proceeding south along the west side of the Little Rouge, beneath two railway bridges, over or through a stream, then down to and across Meadowvale Road and the river, to proceed south to Pearse House and the zoo turnoff from Meadowvale Road.

THE WALK: From the parking lot just off Reesor Road, walk down across the grass to the corner closest to the river. There you'll find a good trail. It passes close to the remains of an old dam. Continuing on through the woods, it's more like a roadway in width. When it narrows, there remains a good, visible trail. At the fork, stay up above, on the less-used path.

Keep an eye on the trail; it becomes elusive, but it does exist. Continue along beside the river on this flat for a while, but at some point you'll have to get up that bank to the right, just a metre or so. Soon you're on the edge of the bank, on a flatland, and the path is beginning to look more like a deer trail.

The trail descends right to the plain, as the river meanders over towards the farm way up on the other side. It's a myth trail along here. As you approach the high bank coming in from the right, go back along the hill a bit until you can find a place to clamber up to the top, preferably climbing at an angle across the face.

At the top you're on a ridge, with the steep bank behind and a gentle slope ahead. Turn to the right and walk along the ridge towards a row of pines ahead. Follow along beside them. Down along the edge there's the remains of an old access or logging road, leading back towards the river. Although it's much over-grown now, there is a passage along the left side. Go down.

On the other side of the hydro right-of-way, turn left downhill towards the river.

At the bottom, walk over towards the river and the bridge, then cross beneath it. Take the path angling up to the right into the evergreens. It levels out and goes across the hill, and eventually you'll be up on top of the bluffs.

Follow a clear but narrow path through some old dead sumac. There's an old bush road coming down from the right. Follow it to the left for a ways, and as you approach a second railway bridge, go down a level to the water's edge.

Just this side of the railway there's a stream, the one warned about in the note at the beginning, and depending on weather conditions and the time of year, it may or may not be a problem. Sometimes there's hardly a hint of a stream, but when there is a stream, there are some stepping stones in it. If it's become a big stream, consider taking off shoes and socks. If, as far as you're concerned, the stream is not crossable, there is a B option. It will take a little more time—it's challenging in terms of following directions, but it's physically easier. Let's look at the A option first.

Option A: Once past the creek, the easiest way across the railway is up and over. But this would be both illegal and dangerous, as traffic is heavy along this line. The other way is to climb up beneath the bridge.

There's an old concrete abutment, and behind it is a row of rails on end, driven down into the soil, tied together with horizontal rails, and back-filled with big chunks of rock. With care, there's a way between the abutment and the rails. From there, carefully climb over the rocks and eventually down the other side.

Finally, however you reach it, you're on the flat ground, 2.5 metres up from the floodplain, beside the river on the other side of the railroad bridge. Another old abutment looms ahead, with a good trail passing between it and the end of the old railbed to the right. Those are the last major scrambles out of the way.

Option B: Go back the way you came as far as that bush road, turn left, and follow it up through a pine plantation to where it begins to swing right. Now turn left, at right angles to the road. There is no pathway so you'll have to brush-bash to the edge of the plantation. When you reach it, to the right there's a grove of sumac. Go there, up on a little ridge. Cross it, and at the other side you'll see a barn, but don't go there.

Turn left past the end of the sumac and work your way through the fallen branches and dog strangling vine to another ridge. Climb it, and ahead is the edge of the ravine cut by the little stream. Congratulations, but don't get too excited: it's a long drop down the side of the ravine. Turn right here and do your best to follow beside the edge, until you come to the place where the stream makes a right-angled turn in front. The ravine is much less high here, and you can easily reach the stream after stepping over the old wire fence. As soon as possible, cross the stream and follow it back downstream towards the tracks.

At the rail line you should see immediately ahead an arched tunnel beneath the embankment. There's at least a metre and a half of clearance, and it's easy to get to the other side. Continue across the gully following the trail there and up the side of the hill, actually a second railway embankment, this one long abandoned. At the top turn left, and follow the trail for a few yards to a trail down the other side. It's steep and can be slippery when wet, so be careful going down. At the bottom, continue to follow the trail until shortly it turns sharply left. When you get into the cedar woods, the trail angles off to the right; ignore it and brush-bash straight ahead until you get down to the water. This where the description of Option B ends.

The other, third option, of course, is to turn around and enjoy your walk back to the beginning; every trail looks different when seen from the opposite direction.

There's no particular trail down here—just follow the easiest course. Some of these trails are streams in wet times. They run on two levels, close to the water and a little higher and further away.

The trail becomes clear and gravelly as you follow it through a dense grove of cedars, across a little stream and up to the Meadowvale Road. Cross it and cross the bridge, and enter the forest on the right between the two cedar trees, portals to a wide, well-used path.

Further along is one of the recent improvements implemented by the Rouge Conservation Authority, a long series of steps leading up the side of the old riverbank. At the top the trail is clear and easily passable, and it wends through a dense grove of saplings and into a wide, open field.

As you approach the rail line, there is a trail leading to the right over to the side of the ravine. Here there's another recently built set of steps down and up the other side, with a boardwalk across the stream in the middle.

When you enter the field, take the path to the left, because it's a good vantage point to look over towards the trees on the far side, the piles of rocks in the middle, and all the grassland in between. Here is a favoured hunting ground for foxes, coyotes, merlins, and red-tailed hawks. If you have binoculars, keep them handy.

Off to the left, that high hill is the Beare Road Sanitary Landfill, now supplying methane gas to the factory-like building up ahead on the other side of the tracks. Soon you'll both hear and see it, as it goes about its business of generating electricity from garbage gas.

In recent years, a lot of work has been done to restore vegetation and habitat. It may seem a little patchy now, but it will quickly spread and blend. When a real road intersects the trail, turn right and follow it down into the valley where it crosses the river. There is rarely vehicular traffic here, but look out for the cyclists and dog walkers, of which there are a goodly number, especially on the weekend.

At the top, walk to the right around the big gate. The house on the left is Pearse House Rouge Conservation Centre, and the end of the walk.

GETTING BACK: If using public transportation walk along the left side of the road and across the bridge towards the zoo, to a bus stop just the other side. The 85 Sheppard bus goes west to the Yonge Subway. If you take the 86 bus at Meadowvale and Sheppard, it goes to Kennedy Subway Station.

If you drove, cross the bridge to the bus stop and get the 85 Sheppard bus to McCowan, transfer to the 129 bus north to Steeles and transfer again to the 53 bus back east to the end of the line. From there it's about a 5-kilometre walk back to the beginning of the walk.

LITTLE ROUGE: EAST SIDE

DISTANCE: 6 kilometres

NOTE: With one optional exception, this is an easy walk until the end, when it is necessary to force a way through shrubs and small trees along the side of a steep hill for perhaps a hundred metres.

GETTING THERE BY PUBLIC TRANSIT: The 85 Sheppard bus runs directly to the zoo from the Yonge. The 86A bus from Kennedy Subway Station goes to Meadowvale Road, where you can transfer to the 85 on weekends. On weekdays, it continues on to the zoo. In either case, leave the bus just before it turns left across the bridge to the zoo.

GETTING THERE BY AUTOMOBILE: Drive to the corner of Sheppard Avenue and Meadowvale Road, turn north, and take the zoo turnoff. At the bridge leading to the zoo on the left, turn right. The road dead-ends, and there is parking space available beside the roadway.

SUMMARY: The walk roughly follows the Rouge Park Old Orchard Trail down the east side of the Little Rouge to Twyn Rivers Drive, then, still on the east side, it follows a variety of trails on down to Kingston Road.

THE WALK: After you get off the bus or lock the car, walk to the east, towards the high hill way over on the horizon. You'll pass a renovated Victorian farmhouse on the right, the Pearse House Rouge Valley Conservation Centre. At the entrance there's a display showing the official hiking trails of Rouge Park; you'll be roughly following the Orchard Trail for a while.

Just after beginning the ascent on the other side towards the Beare Road Land Fill with its weather tower up top, take note of a trail running up the high bank to the right. Best get started—this will be the first climb of the day.

Up top there's a good view all around. You can see the trail stretching out on the other side of the road behind you. To the left there's an electric generating station using landfill gases as fuel, and to the right the old bank drops down to the river. Ahead is an open field, with bushes popping up here and there, and trees at the other end. That's where you're headed.

In time this trail leads into a forest. There's a beaver pond off to the left. Canada geese and other waterbirds often nest in there, so best to leave it alone in June and July and allow them to court, breed and raise their young.

Down in the field where it's relatively clear and flat, the trail goes straight ahead across the flat and then plunges down to the river again.

In time you'll get right down beside the river. There are a lot of big granite boulders here, more than usual along Toronto rivers. Normally most would be buried, but since so much gravel was scraped up and hauled off a few years ago, they're all that's left.

The trail is easily visible. It comes back to the main path and then off again, and rough guardrails have been placed beside sudden bank drop-offs.

When the trail splits, take the less-used one to the right. These secondary trails are all well established and don't disturb existing plantlife.

When the main trail goes left, there's a turnoff to the right, through straight rows of spruce and red pine, planted tree-farm fashion. Walk right down the middle. Past the tree farm the trail goes over to the right. There's a deer trail right along the edge, which you definitely should not take. Later on there is a more civilized trail leaving at right angles out to the right, following around a bow.

The trail turns at a right angle to the left, up a little bank and into the woods. Go straight in to the main trail that crosses to the right towards the road.

For those who are beginning to feel a little weary, or who have spent much of their time looking for birds, taking photos, or just enjoying the place, you could now just turn around and retrace your steps. Or you have the option of walking to the right, down the side of the road to the Rouge Park Vista Trail. That will also take you back to Pearse House by a different route. This walk continues on ahead across Twyn Rivers Road.

The trail on the other side continues on clear and wide as before, heading back towards the river. In time you'll reach a parking lot where you have an Option A, Option B choice.

Option A: This, the less demanding of the two, goes out to the road, turns right and follows up past where a stream pours out into a deep gully, tumbling down towards the river. On the other side of the gully there's a clear trail running down along the top of the bank to the end, where you can pick up the description that follows Option B.

Option B: Begins by taking a dim little trail down to the floodplain from about where the post-and-wire fence starts.

The trail climbs up from the floodplain to the left a bit. Ahead is a fairly high, fairly steep bank, quite difficult when wet. The trail is very clear, and has obviously been used for a long time. At the top there's a deep gully. The trail goes down, across the stream on some rocks, and up the other side, with the help of rocks embedded in the earth. If you are not winded by the end of this, seriously consider entering the Olympics. Follow the trail along the bank to the right to the end (the end of Option A as well).

Take a path to the left, leading about halfway up the side of the hill and across it. The trail is narrow and can be slippery in wet weather—watch your step whatever the conditions. Eventually you do get down to the base of the hill, where it's relatively easy walking. Ease over to the right towards the river, where there's a very clear trail. During spring breakup the river throws up chunks of ice all across this plain, and the marks remain on the trees and bushes throughout the year.

In time the trail leaves the river and begins what becomes a very long meander amongst the riverine growth, extending almost down to Old Kingston Road.

Trees on the slopes and higher ground vary perceptibly from west to east in Toronto ravines, but the riverine growth remains much the same—multi-trunked crack willows and Manitoba maples predominating, with large, sinuous grapevines a frequent accompaniment. They sprawl out to cover as much ground and extract as much nourishment from these poor sandy soils as possible, waiting for the next high water year to wash the old away and give the young a chance to start again. There are no other tree species that grow fast enough in these conditions to compete.

In time you'll come to a place where the old bank drops right down to the river. Up at the top are people's fenced-off backyards. Right up against the fences there's dense young growth, plus the cuttings and debris tossed over the fence by householders. Where the houses end, there's a street allowance you can walk along to get to Kingston Road and the bridge. This description covers one possible route across most of the hillside, up towards that street allowance.

Walk along very close to the river, pushing your way through willow shrubs until you reach the beginning of the high bank and the river swings right. Push straight ahead up the hill to the top of a ridge. The other side goes right back down again in a gully. Travel to the left across the side of the gully for a ways, to an old fallen log. Cross the gully following a deer trail coming down from the left, and climb the other side.

Up at the top you'll be greeted by the remains of an old fallen treehouse.

Continue across the hillside to another gully. Ease up again and then climb towards the backyards, and brush-bash along behind three or four of them to the end. If you get hot, tired and frustrated, sit down and rest for a moment; you're almost there.

At the top, follow one more little gully inland, away from the river, and you'll find yourself in that road allowance. Follow it down towards the street. There's a commercial building to your right. Go over there, across the parking lot, and down the hill to the main street at the traffic lights. You've achieved Kingston Road!

Make one last push across the bridge, on the sidewalk provided, to the entrance to the Glen Rouge Campground. This is probably a good place to sit, eat, and decide what to do next.

The walk described in Rouge Walk 4 goes back up to Pearse House via the Rouge River. That walk's about 4.5 kilometres long and easier than this one. Or, if you walk west along Kingston Road here, it's about 1.5 kilometres up to a bus stop.

GETTING BACK: Those who came by public transportation should cross Sheppard Avenue at the lights and get the 85 bus south, to the end of the line at Rouge Hill, there to transfer to the 54 bus, which will take you to the Lawrence East Station of the LRT.

Those who came by car and left it at Pearse House, catch the 85 B or D bus north. This bus goes to the zoo. Get off just before it makes the left turn over the bridge across Meadowvale. Tell the driver where you want to go.

ROUGE WALK 4
KINGSTON ROAD TO MEADOWVALE

DISTANCE: 4.5 kilometres
NOTE: This is a moderately easy walk: the first half is mostly flat walking along trails, with some hills in the second half.
GETTING THERE BY PUBLIC TRANSPORTATION: Take the 54 bus from Lawrence East Station on the LRT to the end of the line at Rouge Hill, and transfer to either the 85 or 95 to Kingston Road. Check with the driver. Walk east down Kingston Road to the park entrance and parking lot.
GETTING THERE BY AUTOMOBILE: Drive east on Kingston Road past Sheppard East. At the bottom of the hill, to the left, is the entrance to the Glen Rouge Campground. Go in there and park in the parking lot.
SUMMARY: The walk begins at the Glen Rouge Campground and goes up the east side of the Rouge River to Twyn Rivers Drive, following the Rouge Riverside Trail much of the time. It crosses the bridge at Twyn Rivers and continues on up the west side of the river to Meadowvale Road, and the bus stop at Sheppard.

THE WALK: Leave the parking lot by the paved path, and cross the footbridge. Downstream to the right is where the Little Rouge Creek meets the main Rouge River. Across the bridge, turn left along a wide path.

At one time there were horse trails along here, and the main trail is still marked with horse trail signs—a brown post with an orange section at the top. You'll be on and off that trail.

Many trees and shrubs have been planted all along here, the white perforated tubes around their bases intended to support and protect them from browsers and nibblers through their first years. Come along here during a cold winter and you can see what happens when young plants don't have this protection.

The trail splits, the one to the right going up to the Ridge Trail. Stay to the left along the river. Across from the campground, there's a nice little falls. The river and the path meander extensively, and the trail is worn deep, partly because it's old, but also because it's mostly sand and doesn't wear well when horses or trail bikes use it.

Around a sharp riverine zig-zag there's a horse trail post on the left. Beyond that keep an eye out to the left. There's a good-sized, sprawling willow tree with an old, rotten log down behind it, almost up to the trail. Just beyond that, there are a pair of mature spruce trees. There are grooves along the left beside you, and one of them cuts off to the left, between the fallen log and the spruces, across the field towards the river. This old horse trail leads through a recent planting, so be careful where you step. The trail leads closer to the riverbank, through a host of wildflowers and shrubs, and grasses full of bugs in summer months. In the winter, tracks and scats are much easier to see in the snow, away from the dog litter near the main trail.

Cross a field and into trees again. To the left there's a small stream in a very deep ravine. Follow its meanders, until the river itself crosses in front. The apparent stream is actually an overflow channel from the river, filled only in flood times.

At about this same place the main trail goes off to the right. Stay on the secondary one, to the left along the river.

Whenever the trail splits, take the older, deeper one beside the river. In time the horse trail comes in from the right, and the two will marry. You can tell this is the official trail because it's wide, well used, and there are a number of railings at places where one could conceivably walk off into the river.

There's a bit of moderate climbing up here, and the railings are appreciated. Nevertheless you are responsible for your own safety, so watch for places where erosion is undermining the railings themselves, and stay well to the right. Past the railings, follow another secondary trail out beside the river.

At the western Twyn Rivers Road Bridge, it's up the bank and over. Watch it, there's no particular allowance for pedestrians across here, so stay to the left where you can keep an eye on oncoming traffic.

On the other side, walk down the path towards the river, where you continue along the bank, up and down. On the other side you can see the last ten thousand years exposed in the sheer hillside, where layer after layer of sand and clay and gravel, deposited by glaciers and melt waters, are exposed to the world's view.

The trail eases over to the left, to begin the gentle ascent up towards the higher level ahead. Up here you're still travelling roughly parallel to the river, though a few yards back. Continue towards the forested hill ahead.

This is a high, steep old bank where, fortunately, the trail cuts up and across at an angle, making the climb gentler, to the edge of a falloff to the river. Reverse direction, now climbing across the hill's face to the left.

The trail splits, the left branch continuing to climb, and the right one going over to the edge, where there's a great view of the river below. Those without wings had best turn left before reaching the edge. There's a nice clear trail along here, and finally you'll reach a flat field dotted with trees and shrubs.

At a cross trail, climb down to the right towards the river, where there's yet another trail to the left along beside it.

The trail becomes obscure in places, so just pick the easiest way upstream—they all come together in the end. You may have to persuade some shrubs to let you pass in a couple of places. You're still heading uphill, and pretty soon you're back along the edge of a bank, somewhat higher now. At the next trail fork, go right.

The trail coming across this one plunges down to the right, towards the river, and that's the one to follow. Down here there's another clear path, well back from the edge, towards a hydro right-of-way. Closer to the Meadowvale Bridge the path begins a long, gentle curve parallel to the road. When it meets the road, continue along beside it to the corner of Sheppard Avenue, where you can cross to the other side to the bus shelter.

GETTING BACK: For those using public transportation, wait in the shelter until the 85 bus comes along. It will take you first to the corner of Meadowvale and Sheppard, where you can transfer to the 86 to the Kennedy Subway, or continue along Sheppard towards the Yonge Subway.

If you drove, assuming the car was left at the Glen Rouge Campground parking lot, take the 85 A, D, or H bus southeast on Sheppard to Kingston Road. At Kingston Road, walk east down the hill to the parking lot.

If you are completing the loop from the Rouge Valley 4 walk, you'll have to walk back up along Meadowvale to the parking lot at the zoo turnoff near Pearse House. (Yes, if you're exhausted, you can take the bus.)

ROUGE WALK 5
RING AROUND THE ROUGES

DISTANCE: 7 kilometres

NOTE 1: There is no public transport to this walk on Sundays or holidays.

NOTE 2: Once started, there is no access to public transport, although in case of emergency the walk does cross two well-travelled roads.

NOTE 3: There is no trail per se for sections of this route. Walking may be difficult because of dense and lush growth, and there are wet spots. There are some short, steep and briefly difficult climbs, but the openness of the trail and ease of walking improve from beginning to end.

NOTE 4: In summer make sure to wear slacks or pants of some kind—there's an abundance of poison ivy and stinging nettles.

GETTING THERE BY PUBLIC TRANSPORTATION: Take the Bloor Subway and LRT extension east to Scarborough City Centre Station, and then take the 131 Nugget bus to the corner of Morningview and Old Finch Road.

GETTING THERE BY AUTOMOBILE: Since the walk description begins at the bus stop, best find an off-road spot close to the junction of Old Finch and Sewells Road. It's a fairly long walk back, so why not leave the car at the subway and take the bus?

SUMMARY: The walk goes east from the bus stop along Old Finch Road to Sewells Road, then north to the bridge across the Rouge. It follows along the Rouge west and north, to an abandoned railway right-of-way paralleling the current CP rail line, then west to the Little Rouge. It then follows the Little Rouge to Meadowvale Road, and turns up the hill, away from the bridge towards the school. Taking the pathway through the vacant lot beside the school and then from the back of the schoolyard down to Little Rouge Creek, it follows along the river to the roadway leading to the zoo.

THE WALK: To begin, a word in the interest of harmonious relations. Although all the land described here has been designated as parkland, bear in mind that some of it, for instance the railway and the farms on both sides of it, is privately owned. The rules are unclear, so use discretion and sensitivity, and stick to the trail.

Once off the bus, walk along the north side of Old Finch to Sewells Road, and turn left. As you're walking down Sewells there's not an awful lot of room between the bank and the paved road, so keep as far left as you can and walk single file. At the bottom of the hill, Old Finch Road begins again, and leads off to the right towards the zoo. Stay on Sewells, continuing around the curve.

Just before the bridge, there's a bronze plaque to the left, set in concrete. It is worth reading. Again, be cautious crossing the bridge. It's strong enough, but it's not very wide. Walk single file on the left side.

You're now on the north bank of the Rouge River. This completes the most dangerous part of the walk and introduces the most challenging section.

Step over the guardrail on the left, and look for a path down the bank to the river; there is one there. It can be slippery, so make sure you're holding on to something as you descend, and look out for the old wire fence.

If there are hints of a trail down here, it's most probably an animal track. There's nothing wrong with following animal tracks, as long as they're going where you want to go. Just remember that a raccoon only needs about 30 centimetres of headroom, a deer only about a metre.

There are two levels beside the river. There's the floodplain level just above the river itself, and then a second one a metre higher up. Generally the lower level presents easier passage, but it can be very difficult going in mid-summer when dog strangling vines proliferate, and the purple loosestrife and all the other plants grow thick and high.

You're going to be pretty well on your own for picking the best route, but the notes here will give you some idea of what to expect.

There are many foot-soaking spots, so best stay away from the cattails unless you're wearing waterproof shoes. In summer there's a demarcation line between types of vegetation, and often following this line will provide the easiest passage possible. It's generally about 6 metres back from the water.

Up on the next level there are many boggy patches also. There are lots of poplar and aspen trees and numerous berry-bearing bushes and shrubs attracting a variety of birds.

Switch levels as opportunities present themselves. Generally, the lower level is more passable than the upper. The plus side of summer travel along here is that the views are gorgeous. Purple and gold flowers prevail, standing out from the countless shades of green. Patches of gravel appear from time to time in low water periods, but usually the vegetation comes right to the water's edge.

There's an open area: open because the soil is so stony it resembles a rock farm.

As the river turns again to the right, you'll see a line of trees running along the top of the far bank. On this side you'll come to an even larger field. Eventually it slowly draws to a pointy end, to the left, closer to the river. If you go to the end, you can climb the steep little bank into the trees—it's actually quite open in here. Once this was easy walking, but now, after the invasion of dog strangling vine, walking can be really hard work. Take it slow and easy, and rest often.

When you reach the railroad bridge spanning the valley it might be a good time to take a break. Have a snack and watch the belted kingfisher belt on by beneath the bridge span.

Looming behind you is the end of an old railway embankment, the base of your path for the next third of the walk. You can climb up on a path to the right, on one straight ahead, or go up in between the old and new embankments. Whichever you choose, get to the top.

Up top there's a good view of the tree farm, with straight rows of plants of various ages and stages, and piles of compost. On the left is the rail line and beyond it a farm. For about three quarters of the year there's a trail visible along here, and all year it's flat and level.

The raspberry bushes return a fine reward for your efforts during a couple of weeks in season, but are an impediment the rest of the time. They're not terribly thick, but it's no place for shorts.

Next is the first of a number of cuts across the embankment, created to drain the gully between this and the other embankment. It's steep on both sides, so proceed with caution. There is lots of vegetation to hold on to.

There's a huge apple tree, spreading majestically across the whole width of the embankment in the fullness of its health and vigour. It invites you to make a small detour to the left. Commercial apple trees are smaller now so that the fruit is easier to pick. This one is reminiscent of former glories.

The raised embankment becomes a sunken slot. When this was active railbed it was maintained as level as possible, with the low spots filled in and the high points knocked down.

As you come up to Sewells Road, bear to the left and descend through the cut, down a steep little slide to the roadside. Look carefully in both directions—it's hard for oncoming traffic to see you. Cross and climb. Turn to the right to get back on the top of the embankment. You may have to push your way through the young trees in places.

A SMALL TRIBUTARY OF THE LITTLE ROUGE, NORTH OF PEARCE HOUSE. NOW, A CENTURY AGO, OR A THOUSAND YEARS AGO? A MOMENT OUT OF TIME IN THE HIDDEN COUNTRY.

There's another cut across the path. It too is short and steep, with lots of vegetation to hold on to. Further along there's a stretch where some sort of vehicle has been driven occasionally, resulting in a path more open than usual. Yet another cut, but this one is shallow and easily descended and climbed.

At last the vehicle track turns right into the woods. It becomes boggy down to the right; in spring it may even be flooded for a while.

Reesor Road is much less heavily used than Sewells, and the visibility in both directions is good. The embankment seems to disappear on the other side because the level is the same as that of the surrounding land. But it's there, just keep walking parallel to the railway line.

When you reach the next cut, you've come too far. As you approach the cut, on your right there's a gully beginning to drop off, and growing progressively deeper. When the white farm house on the other side of the field is at about right angles to the path, it's time to turn right and cross over to the field. Turn left and follow the edge on the field side down to the corner. Continue parallel to the rail line, to a clear trail with a couple of square trail markers on it—one white with blue, the other yellow with red. Continue along this trail into a cedar wood.

The trails in here are used extensively by students from the Hillside Outdoor Education School over on Meadowvale Road. During the school term you may meet a group of them with a teacher. If you've found anything of interest, do ask the teacher if it's all right to share. If you're interested, the kids probably will be too.

Continue on between two stands of cedars across a field. The trail edges to the left, and soon you're at the top of a short bank on the edge of another cedar wood.

When the trail bends to the right and forks, take the one to the right. It leads to a steep little climb to Meadowvale Road. Cross to the other side of the road, turn right, and up the hill. Just before reaching the school building, turn left and cross the field. Follow the trail down the hill from the school.

Further down, the trail splits. Take the one to the right. At the bottom there's a well-trodden path through this woodland.

In time you'll come to the Valley Halla estate, currently housing the administration services of the Rouge Park. The house is to the right, and below it is what appears to be the weathered white rail of an ancient racetrack. The trail leads right up to that rail, and follows it on the north side past the building entrance. After the fence, the trail continues on towards the top edge of the field, towards a gravel road. It jogs to the right and then joins another road leading up a hill to the left.

Almost immediately turn left to take a trail towards the river. Follow the river around to a fork and take the one to the left down closer to river level. There are banks of gravel and sand to the left, the remains of quarry operations down here when this whole valley was opened as a resource to road builders. Climbing up from this lower level, the trail runs into an old abandoned roadway. Follow it to the right to the paved road to the Beare Road Landfill. Turn right uphill towards Pearse House. Continue on past and across the bridge over Meadowvale Road to a TTC bus stop.

GETTING BACK: If no car is waiting to meet you in the parking space beside Pearse House, you can take either of two buses that stop here. The 85 Sheppard East will carry you first to Sheppard, where you can transfer to the 86 bus, or continue due west to the Yonge Subway. On weekdays, the 86 Scarborough goes to Kennedy Subway Station and the Bloor Subway.

INTERLUDE 6

THE NIGHT HAZEL BLEW INTO TOWN

There was one event, which more than any other has both physically affected the shape of today's ravines and changed the public and institutional attitude to them. That was Hurricane Hazel.

On the evening of October 16, 1954, all hell broke loose on Toronto. Certainly it must have seemed so to the eighty-one men, women and children who lost their lives that night in Hurricane Hazel.

Earlier in the day, between 15 and 18 centimetres of rain fell; the previous record was less than 10 centimetres. It was driven by winds clocked at 90 kilometres per hour, with gusts of over 110. On the 800 square kilometres of the Humber Watershed alone, from the Oak Ridges Moraine down to Lake Ontario, that meant that in a 48-hour period, 182 billion litres of water, weighing 182 million tonnes, hit the ground, flowing. The bulk of that fell in the last 12 hours.

It had been raining off and on for a week; the earth was saturated—it could hold no more. The only place all that water could go was downhill, and the most obvious route was through the city's ravines and rivers.

Trains were delayed, stopped or toppled off washed-out tracks. Passengers were marooned, as were many trying to drive along roads which in moments became lakes. Some drowned.

Although damage was worst on the Humber, in all the valleys, roads, railroad tracks, bridges, sewer and other utility lines, trees, cars and sometimes houses and people were swept away by torrents the likes of which had not been seen in recorded history.

Betty Kennedy described the night vividly in her book *Hurricane Hazel.*

As the rains fell and were funnelled into the streams and creeks that drain into the lake, the streams became raging rivers, and the bridges over them suddenly became death traps. Against the backdrop of those many bridges, a series of grim and deadly dramas were played out in the hours of darkness. Howling winds, the sinister roar of rivers on the rampage ("like a fast-moving freight train" John Ridpath remembers, the sound of the Humber River still in his ears), shrieks and cries for help, shouted instructions from would-be rescuers, all punctuated a black night made eerie with improvised light from torches and truck headlights.

Surrounding towns and villages were hit just as hard, were just as viciously smashed, and were just as thoroughly devastated. Many people had lived on their river for half a century—they were used to spring floods. At times some had even chosen to leave home for a day or two until the worst was past, but never in living memory had there been so much, or so fast.

After they peaked in the early hours of the morning, it didn't take the waters long to subside either. Many people, even some living close by the ravines, didn't really believe the news they heard on the radio on Saturday morning. But it was real.

Betty Kennedy, describing Raymore Drive on the Humber, where sixteen homes had been washed away and thirty-two men, women and children died, noted that, "All the familiar land-marks were missing: the trees, the other houses, the footbridge. Instead there was rubble, huge slabs of concrete, literally tons of mud and silt and bricks and boards. There was no sign of vegetation. All the gardens and trees were buried or had been washed away."

The little valleys, the stream beds, the ravines, had been scoured, purged and flushed.

Ironically, just the day before, Air Vice-Marshall T. A. Lawrence had been trying valiantly to cobble together some sort of emergency defence unit to coordinate municipal services such as fire, police and ambulance. He had resigned his position in utter frustration over the endless carping and haggling between levels of government about who would pay for what. It was 1979 before Metro had a fully documented emergency plan.

However, sometimes a strong dose of reality will effect change when nothing else has been successful. Within four days officials organized the first of many meetings to ensure nothing like this could happen again, or at least to prevent such horrendous loss of life and property. Various levels of government and public groups met, talked, and set processes in motion, and the Metropolitan and Region Conservation Authority was born.

Its mandate covers 3,700 square kilometres of land and water, including all the watersheds of all the streams entering Lake Ontario, from Etobicoke Creek to Carruthers Creek, and the shores of Lake Ontario within the boundaries of Pickering, Ajax and Metro Toronto.

Ten years later, the Claireville Dam and Reservoir on the West Humber was completed and became operational. Thousands of hectares of floodplain and valley lands had been purchased, and controls formulated to guide future developments right back up to the Oak Ridges Moraine. And there was a good flood warning system in place. As the process continued the G. Ross Lord Dam was constructed near the top of the city, and two smaller ones at Milne and Stouffeville, north of the city, were also completed.

As time passed, the authority broadened its concern into the realm of conservation because, on reflection, it realized that the two processes were inseparable. As scientists increased their understanding of ecological processes, they began to understand that more benefits would accrue, and the same level of control would be available in most instances, if native trees and shrubs were allowed to grow on stream banks. Much of the conservation work currently under way under the auspices of the authority and city agencies centres upon undoing two centuries of ignorant mismanagement.

Public groups have always been involved formally or otherwise in conservation work, and that continues. Clean Up the Don or Humber Days are still needed, and will be as long as some few look at the ravines as garbage dumps. Friends of the Rouge have done outstanding work to preserve that watershed. More importantly, no laws or regulations are unchangeable, and the pressure to make a profit from these lands is quiet but hugely powerful and unrelenting. Present plans to bring back and preserve nature in the city will only be realized when ordinary people, with their hugely divergent range of interests, want to keep in touch with the rest of the universe stretching out beyond the parking lot.

AFTERWORD

Is that all there is?

In Toronto we are blessed not only with the ravine lands, but also with a host of small neighbourhood parks. They may have a streamlet running through, or the gully where one once flowed. They may be only a scrap of land set aside by planning rules as "park," simply a piece of turf with a regulation group of playground pieces for young children. But even in a vacant lot, awaiting the erection of the next highrise, there's life for those who have the interest to stop for a moment and look.

Toronto Parks have created Discovery Walks pamphlets for Garrison Creek, Don Valley Hills and Dales, Northern Ravines and Gardens, Central Ravines, Belt Line and Gardens, Eastern Ravine and Beaches, Western Ravines and Beaches, and Humber Wetlands. They are available in libraries or from city hall, and include route maps and much useful information.

Two other walks to seriously consider are the Toronto Islands, reachable from the ferry docks at the foot of Bay Street, and the Leslie Spit, or Tommy Thompson Park, beginning at the foot of Leslie Street. It's available only on the weekends, as it's still under construction during the week. But it's an outstanding example of what happens when humans refrain from "helping" the natural world.

There are a number of maps available, but no one single map is likely to have all the information you want. Get the TTC Ride Guide. It's free, but you may need your pocket magnifier to read it. There's also one published in the Yellow Pages directory; pretty good but hard to carry. There are a couple of different street maps available—look for the one with the largest print. A Metro Cycling map can be very useful, because where there's a paved cycling path beside a watercourse, there's often a trail through the rough on the other side. Unfortunately, you'll often need all three to find where you want to go and how to get there by public transport.

If you find you have an interest in the natural world, get yourself a field guide. Any kind on any subject will do. Use it at least three times, and you'll begin to experience that lift of recognition that comes from establishing familiarity. The library and mega bookstores are the best places to look first. And if you enjoy books as well as nature, there are more than fifty very good used book shops in town; great places to spend a cold and sleety December afternoon.

If you find you enjoy the walks and the wildlife, you might want to contact the Toronto Field Naturalists. They are a group of people who, like yourself, are developing an understanding of the natural world. There is expertise indeed, but most members simply enjoy exploring and learning. The stated purpose of this organization is to, "encourage the preservation of our natural heritage." Their walks are all within the city and cover both the wild beauty of the ravines and city streets, where there are natural or historical points of interest. Leaders are knowledgeable, and there's usually time to stop, look and listen. In addition, they are the source of a number of excellent publications, containing a wealth of information about life in the ravines. Contact them directly for specific titles and prices.

To push your understanding further, use the Internet. If you are not connected at home, try the facilities available in most of Toronto's public libraries. Hint: call first and book ahead, Internet access is still a scarce resource in the libraries, and the few computers available are heavily used. There's a wealth of information available, and it is only likely to expand with time.

There's so much more to the world than glass and concrete and lawns. Get out. Get in. Enjoy.

As our species continues to increase in number, we will push the other inhabitants of our environment further and further away, until, like them, our days of decline come in their turn. As we close ourselves off from the rest of the world in our constructs of glass and steel, it's important for the maintenance of our humanity that some retain intimate contact with the rest of that world.

Sometime in the far distant future we may evolve beyond our present forms, but until that time, the best of what we are seems to come from that very world we're trying to bury. It is my hope that you will find some of the joy, the laughter, the fascination, the awe and the peace and re-creation that I have over the years in the ravines around us.

M. S.